ERROR ANALYSIS IN ENGLISH

ERROR ANALYSIS IN ENGLISH

By

Dr. Sobhana Nandyal Panduranga
Assistant Professor
Department of English
College of Science & Arts, Samtah Campus
Jazan University, Jizan
Kingdom of Saudi Arabia

DPH

DISCOVERY PUBLISHING HOUSE PVT. LTD.
INDIA

Published by:
Namit Wasan
DISCOVERY PUBLISHING HOUSE PVT. LTD.
4383/4B, Ansari Road, Darya Ganj
New Delhi-110 002 (India)
Phone : +91-11-23279245, 43596064-65
Fax : +91-11-23253475
E-mail: discoverypublishinghouse@gmail.com
namitwasan9@gmail.com
sales@discoverypublishinggroup.com
web : www.discoverypublishinggroup.com

First Edition: **2017**

ISBN: 978-93-5056-869-9

Error Analysis in English

Printed at:
Infinity Imaging Systems
Delhi

Foreword

I am glad to write the foreword to the important book on *Error Analysis in English* written by Dr. Sobhana Nandyal. In fact, Dr. Sobhana has been my former colleague and is my great friend. Error analysis refers to the finding out and analysing various kinds of errors that occur in a language context. Error analysis is an essential problem solving process by careful research in case of the learners of English as a Second Language and hence this problem gains prominence in the contemporary Indian society or in any other society in any other parts of the globe. Error analysis involves the study of the types and causes of language errors. In that Bussmann (1996) indicated that errors can be classified on as per six bases, that is, *modality*, in terms of level of proficiency in speaking, writing, reading, listening; *linguistic levels*, that is, pronunciation, grammar, vocabulary, style; *form*, that is, omission, insertion, substitution; *type*, such as, systematic errors/errors in competence vs. occasional errors/errors in performance; *cause* like interference, interlanguage; and *norm versus system*.

Though error analysis forms part of linguistics, the current text has examined it from the view of English teaching methodology. The problems faced by English teacher trainers as also by English teacher trainees in the Indian context form important components of this report. The author made lots of efforts in analysing the errors committed by English teacher trainees and giving solutions to overcome such problems. Dr. Sobhana has followed the conventions in Error Analysis research in terms of - collecting samples of learner language, identifying the errors, describing the errors, explaining the errors, and evaluating/correcting the errors. The sample selected, methodology used, tools used, and the findings of the study are useful for the future investigators in this area of research.

Hence, I am confident that the present book rendered by Dr. Sobhana is useful to English language teachers, English language trainers, school students, teacher trainees, and policy planners. It is of interest to general readers from non-English speaking communities also. She did a great service in writing this book especially in the contemporary arena of English teaching and learning in India which poses lots of difficulties for an honest teacher because the subject English is a second language for the learners here. I wish that many more such useful books would be rendered by her in future for the benefit of the learners of English as a second language.

Prof. D.Srinivas Kumar
Head, Department of Education and
HRD & Former Dean
Dravidian University, Srinivasavanam
Kuppam - 517 426
Andhra Pradesh, (India)

Preface

Error analysis, a branch of applied linguistics, emerged in the sixties to demonstrate that learner errors were not only because of the learner's native language but also due to universal learning strategies. It is a reaction to contrastive analysis theory, which considered language transfer as the basic process of second language learning as what behaviorist theory suggested. Error analysis looks for, why learners make errors. It also determines the common difficulties in learning and help teachers to develop materials for remedial teaching. Errors provide feedback about the effectiveness of teachers' teaching techniques and show which aspects need further attention. Error analysis enables teachers to find out the sources of errors and take pedagogical precautions towards them. Thus, the analysis of learner language has become an essential need to overcome some questions and propose solutions regarding different aspects. Correction of errors is as important as identification and description of them for the treatment of errors. The sources and the kinds of errors are determiners for feedback. In conclusion, the inevitable existence of errors has led researchers to study them and find out the natural steps for language learning. The findings of error analysis function as a facilitator in language teaching in many ways only when the teacher is aware of them and able to make use of them in the teaching process appropriately, effectively and efficiently.

The present research project is devoted to introduce what error analysis is and what sort of relationship it has with language teaching and what contribution it provides for English language teaching and learning. The investigator being a teacher educator in Methods of teaching English found it worthwhile to undertake a research study to identify the errors of B.Ed., trainees while writing in English and suggested a remedial program to overcome errors and improve their writing skills in English. This study is concerned with error analysis and its contribution to English language teaching at both linguistic and methodological levels. The present study is, therefore an ardent effort in this direction.

The information in this book *"Error Analysis in English"* has been organized in the following manner:

Chapter - 1, a broad view of the research study has been presented. The significance of language, language skills, importance of learning English, English for communication, glory of English in India, the factors which affect English language learning and the present scenario of English language teaching have been discussed in detail.

Chapter - 2, an intensive review of related literature has been undertaken to have a conceptual clarity of the subject matter of the current study.

Chapter - 3, the problem has been stated with its objectives and hypotheses.

Chapter - 4, methods employed in the selection of the sample, construction of the tools, collection of data, statistical techniques used in the analysis have been given.

Chapter - 5, the analysis of the data and discussion there on are depicted.

Chapter - 6, major findings, conclusions arrived at and implications of the study have been presented. Certain aspects for further exploration have also been suggested.

Bibliography shows the books, articles and journals that have been consulted and the dissertations that have been cited.

Appendix - 1 comprises of the writing package that has been used in the intervention program to train the students.

Appendix - 2 contains the data gathering tool (Test in Writing) that has been administered on the sample of the research study.

This book provides access to indispensable material for researchers in the field of error analysis. In general, it is well illustrated and an informative reference book. It will cater to the needs of teachers, teacher educators, educational planners, administrators and research scholars.

My sincere thanks to Prof. D. Srinivas Kumar, School of Education & HRD, Dravidian University, Kuppam for his encouragement and constructive suggestions in successful completion of the study.

I express my deep sense of gratitude to Prof. S. Subramanyam, Head, Dept. of Education, Annamacharya College of Education, New Boyanapalli, Rajampet, for his valuable guidance, encouragement and was a source of inspiration to undertake this study.

I specially acknowledge Dr. M.A. Jeyarajan, Dr. V.R. Narayanaswami, Dr. S.Jagadesan, Dr. N. Murugaiyan, Dr. N. Krishnaswamy, Dr. T. Sriraman, Dr. Sujatha Mukiri, Dr. Shivendra, K. Verma, and Dr. Hemalatha Nagarajan for having utilized their material in the preparation of the writing package to train the sample of this research study. The sample has displayed a remarkable improvement in their performance while writing in English after the intervention program. I also acknowledge Dr. G. Manivannam, Dr. Sangeeta and Dr. Surender, Dr. S. Dhillon and Dr. Xavier for having consulted their resources in the preparation of the research project report. I am very much indebted to all the authors for their valuable resources.

I am thankful to all students of the School of Education & HRD for sparing their valuable time. I will be failing in my duty if I don't thank Ms. Sheetal (M.Ed. Student) who has helped me in administering the tests.

The success of one's academic venture depends to a large extent on the co-operation, sacrifices and moral contributions of many people. I am therefore; very much indebted to my parents, daughters and my husband without whose co-operation this academic endeavor would have never seen the light of the day.

Dr. Sobhana Nandyal Panduranga

Abstract

Error analysis is the field that deals with the actual errors and tries to describe them in linguistic terms and explain some of the probable sources of errors which provide an understanding of the underlying process of second language acquisition. The purpose of this current study was to assess, describe and analyze the errors committed by ESL learners of Dravidian University. The investigator has followed the methodology of error analysis suggested by Corder (1973). It involved recognition of errors, description of errors and explanation of errors in terms of their sources and evaluation of errors. For this purpose, a test in writing has been administered on the sample of the study. The participants comprised of 100 B.Ed., trainees who opted different optional at B.Ed., level in the School of Education and HRD, Dravidian University. The Pre test Post test design has been used to conduct the experiment. The data was analyzed in percentages on the frequency of errors. The statistical techniques that were applied for the analysis of data were χ^2,'t' test and ANOVA. The students have committed interlingual and intralingual errors while writing in English. The findings from this study indicated that the participants do not have the desired knowledge in morphology and syntax of English language to perform well in writing tasks. Findings of error analysis function as facilitator in language teaching in many ways only if the teacher is aware of them and able to make use of them in the teaching process appropriately. English teachers should try to know the reasons behind students' problems and find out solutions to overcome problems while writing in English. They are requested to take steps to diagnose the different kinds of errors committed by students so as to improve their proficiency in English. They should take the responsibility to motivate the students in a way to create interest towards learning English which should be a stress free environment. Orientation programs and refresher courses should be conducted to all the English language teachers in schools under the jurisdiction of the university.

Key Words: Error analysis, interlingual errors, intralingual errors, ESL.

Contents

1

Introduction

LANGUAGE

A language is a systematic means of communication by the use of sounds or conventional symbols. It is the code used to express and communicate to others. It is the mental faculty or power of vocal communication. It is a system for communicating ideas and feelings using sounds, gestures, signs or marks. Any means of communicating ideas, specifically, human speech, the expression of ideas by the voice and sounds articulated by the organs of the throat and mouth is a language. Language is a means of communicating thoughts and feelings especially to impart them to others.

Language is something specific to humans, that is to say it is the basic capacity that distinguishes humans from all other living beings. Language therefore remains potentially a communicative medium capable of expressing ideas and concepts as well as moods, feelings and attitudes.

Language Skills

The purpose of a language is communication, which means that language helps a person formulate one's thoughts and encode it for the benefit of others who decode it. If one has to communicate proficiently in a language, one needs to master the four basic language skills- Listening, Speaking, Reading and Writing. Listening and reading are known as receptive skills as the receiver receives the information from the source. Speaking and writing are known as productive skills or expressive skills as the information is to be produced/expressed in oral or written modes of the language. Listening and speaking are intimately related to each other, though one is recognition or receptive skill and the other is a productive or active skill. Both the skills depend almost entirely on the learner's knowledge of pronunciation of words and the articulation of sounds in the language. In a similar way, reading is a receptive skill where as writing is a productive skill. Both reading and writing are related to each other, as reading serves as an input for writing.

Language skills can be acquired only through practice. In case of mother tongue the learner gets sufficient scope for practice from the environment.

The learner practices the language without being conscious of the fact that one is learning a highly complex code. Teachers, parents, playmates and others teach the child language without any deliberate effort and supply models for imitation and examples for formulation of the ad-hoc rules about the language.

In case of second language, particularly when it happens to be a foreign language like English, the natural resources are not available to the learner. In such an environment there is some pressure on the learners which can be overcome by providing a stimulating environment in the school/college by enabling them to adopt appropriate strategies. The classroom activities must provide sufficient motivation and scope to practice the target language.

Listening

Familiarity with the English sound system and ability to articulate English sounds prepare the students for listening to English utterances with understanding. Listening precedes speaking and paves a way to develop oral fluency and accuracy. Listening ability involves auditory comprehension and this can be cultivated through listening practice. In Indian context, the students are hampered by inadequate range of words and phrases, inability to maintain attention, inability to understand pronunciation and inability to understand fast speech.

Speaking

Listening should precede practice in speaking. The students should be able to recognize a sound at the phonological level before they attain an ability to produce it. But listening does not lead naturally on to speaking and oral fluency in communication unless listening is followed by practice at both the grammatical and lexical levels. So, listening-attention should be sharpened with particular emphasis on grammatical and lexical items. Listening is a receptive skill like reading and speaking is productive skill like writing. Just as sharpening reading-attention benefits writing, sharpening listening-attention benefits speaking. The students lack knowledge in the application of proper stress on syllables and words or absence of stress at all. They get confused between sound and meaningful contrasts, fail to discriminate between long and short vowels or diphthongs, a tendency to aspire when not required, interference of the phonological system of the mother tongue of the learner and misapplication of lexis and idioms.

Reading

Reading like listening is a decoding process. But it is a very complex process involving many physical, intellectual and often emotional reactions. Moreover, it entails the ability to recognize graphic symbols and their corresponding vocal sounds. It is impossible to learn to read without this ability, which extends to understand complex groups of sounds called words, phrases, sentences, paragraphs and chapters. Reading becomes meaningful only if one gets at the meaning behind the graphic symbols through one's ability to recognize the semantic content of the graphic symbols and the sounds they represent. The students need to develop the ability to read fast and with good comprehension of texts that are easy in language and subject matter or difficult texts that are familiar, ability to read slowly but with excellent comprehension, difficult text on professional, academic and technical subjects in which one has special interests and requires specialized knowledge, ability to skim and dip, ability to use works of reference and ability to size up a book quickly.

Writing

Learning to write is not merely learning to put down on paper. The conventional symbols of writing system represent the utterances one has in mind, purposeful selection and organization of ideas, facts and experiences.

Writing is different from speaking and it aims at compactness and precision in expression as well as grammatical, idiomatic and orthographic accuracy and in that conventions of writing tend to be less flexible than those of speech. Therefore, learning to write is learning to use grammar with ease and facts in some sequential order as tools. In other words, writing is a thinking process, which involves both accuracy and fluency. Many of the Indian students lack proper writing skills as they have inadequate lexical range, grammatical faults, misspellings, faulty punctuation and misapplication of words and phrases in different contexts.

Importance of Learning English

Of all the languages in the world today, English deserves to be regarded as a world language. It is the world's most widely spoken language. A very important reason for regarding English as a world language is that the world's knowledge is enshrined in English. English is being learnt and used all over the world not out of any imposition but through the realization that it has certain inherent advantages. Today, the compulsions of learning English in India are no longer merely political and national but scientific, technological and international. English has a special place in India. This is not merely because English is a world language but because of historical associations, it has entered the fabric of India's culture. India should move and establish channels of communication with other nations. Perhaps, in this present technological world there is no better means of communication other than English. Hence, English has attained the status of a link language. English is needed not only for operational purposes, but also for identifying ourselves with those who use the language in India and abroad. In an era where the status of English has been raised to that of a link language in the present-day global village, there has been a growing awareness of the value and importance of learning the language in its true form and manner. It is in this respect that the proper development of the English language skills gains an immediate attention for its apt and adequate nourishment.

There are two kinds of motivation to learn English. (1) "When any one learns a foreign language instrumentally s/he needs it for operational purposes" i.e., to be able to read books in the new language and to be able to communicate with other speakers of that language. For example, the tourist, the salesmen, the science students are clearly motivated to learn English instrumentally. (2) "When any one learns a foreign language in an integrated manner s/he needs it for integrative purpose" i.e., the person wants to feel at home in that language. The increasing awareness of the importance in the world compels to learn English both for instrumental purposes and integrative purposes, for special or specific purposes and for widening one's intellectual horizon.

English for Communication

The teachers of English should undertake the task of giving a sound knowledge of English to their students keeping in mind a radically enlarged view of the function of English in India as well as the world today. The emphasis must be on good English and not on English just as 'a library language' or as 'a language working knowledge of which can help get information and knowledge from books written in English' without having the ability to use the language for intelligent discussion and communication. So, one cannot dispute that the Indian student must learn the grammar of English in the sense that the sentences one produces must confirm to English patterns in the accepted model; nor can dispute that speech habits should be intelligible and acceptable enough to suit the occasions for which utterances are intended.

If English has to be used for communication by an Indian student, one should achieve the competence in the language to suit the occasion and also to listen with understanding to other speakers and interpret them to the full. Geoffrey Broughton (1980) is right when he observes "As far as the foreign learner is concerned, the history of language teaching shows emphasis on a very limited range of competence which has been called 'Classroom English' or 'Textbook English' and has often proved less than useful for any 'real' communicative purpose. That is to say, as long as the use of English for academic purposes in restricted areas like commerce or administration, a limited command of the language chiefly in the written form, was found reasonable and adequate. But in modern times, the world has shrunk and in many cases interpersonal communication is now more vital than academic usage. It is now important for the learner to be equipped with the command of English which allows one to express oneself in speech or writing in a much greater variety of contexts. What is required is that the teachers of English should lay emphasis on the communicative needs of the students while teaching them English for communication.

The objective of teaching English in India is not to produce a Sarvepalli Radhakrishnan or a Swami Vivekananda, but to equip young generations to transact their professional life which is predominantly English speaking.

Glory of English Language in India

Manivannan, G. (2006) has clearly stated the importance of English language and it has been presented under the glory of English language in India. The historical circumstances of India have given the Indians an easy access to master English language, and innumerable opportunities for advancement in the field of science and technology. Many Indians have become so skilled in English language and have won many international awards for creative and comparative literatures during the last few years. An Indian author, Arundhati Roy, won the prestigious booker prize for her book "The God of Small Things". Her book was sold all over the globe.

Over the years, English language has become one of the principal assets in getting a global leadership for books written by Indian authors and for films made by Indians in English language. A famous Indian movie producer Shekhar Kapoor's film "Elizabeth" has got several nominations for Oscar Awards. It does not require any further support to establish the advantage English language has brought to us at the international level.

English language is an aid in the commercial transactions throughout the globe. English is the language of the latest business management in the world and Indian proficiency in English has brought laurels to many Indian business managers. English is a means not only for international commerce but also for inter-state commerce and communication.

In India, people going from North to South for education or business mostly communicate in English, which has become a link language. Keeping this in view, the Parliament has also recognized English as an official language in addition to Hindi. All the facts of history and developments in present day India underline the continued importance of learning English in addition to vernaculars.

Some of the states of India are witnessing popular increase in public demand for teaching of English language from the primary classes. Most of the schools in the country have English as the sole or additional medium of instruction.

Factors which Affect English Language Learning

Motivation plays a very significant role in language learning. The child has intrinsic motivation in the process of acquisition of mother tongue to establish identity with other children. In the case of second language learning the learner gives more importance to meaning of utterances in order to communicate more than the child who is acquiring mother tongue. Hence, classroom activity should be geared to motivate learners and ensure effective communication in the target language. So, drilling of sentence patterns should be done in which the learner understands every lexical item. It is a well-known fact that what is learned is better retained when the language involved is meaningful. It is easy to learn sentences that are semantically and structurally well formed, sentences whose meaning and grammatical structure are easily acceptable to the learner.

In second language learning the duration of exposure towards second language is a critical factor. In India English is taught as a second language in schools and colleges for six hours in a week. Perhaps the duration is hardly adequate and the courses are spread over years. The two facts make it difficult to create a sustained interest and inculcate a sense of progress and achievement in our students. However, the long period of exposure to English, though intermittent and not intensive, enable students to have a certain degree of familiarity with sentence patterns, words, and phrases in the language which, with some more continuous contact with the language strengthens the ability to write it though not to speak it.

English as a second language classroom is a very crucial factor in second language learning to take up classroom activity. It includes the number of students in a class, the physical arrangements for the class, teaching materials such as chalk, blackboard, audio-visual aids, library, etc. It is very important that second language classes are of the right size. A class consisting of fifty or more becomes difficult, as individual attention cannot be paid to students. One of the reasons why teaching English in India does not leave the desired impact on the student is that the class is overcrowded for the teacher to do any worthwhile job.

The availability of teaching materials and audio-visual aids can certainly make the teaching of English in India quite effective. Audio-visual aids are an integral part of the learning situation and are as important as the blackboard and chalk. In India teaching English is affected by inadequate and poor availability of resources. Though English learning begins in the third Standard (in the non-English medium schools in most of the states) and goes on till the end of the second year of college education, yet the standard of English reached by students in general is poor because of inadequacies related to teaching aids and other environmental factors.

Students and teacher are the two vital factors in a second language learning situation. The teacher has problems to tackle when faced with the task of teaching a class of students who show varying capacities of assimilation. In India even at the college level a large number of students have to be given elementary lessons in the language and as well as to the students who have a better standard. They feel that the lessons and methods adopted are not appropriate to their age and lose interest. In such situations the teacher will have to convince the students and sustain interest. Some of the students are weakly motivated owing to their social and family background. Then, the teacher must stimulate and sustain motivation. The variations that exist in the standards of students in the same class pose other problems too. Individual attention to students can remedy the situation to a great extent. But this is possible only if the class is of small size. A study of the entry behavior of each and every student is not practicable; nor is it possible because of the difficulties that come in the way of deciding on objectives in terms of desired terminal behavior in each of the four skills. What is perhaps possible is to assess the average competence of the class and then to impart systematic instruction taking in to account the length of course in terms of teaching time, time at the disposal of the student for personal work, amount of exposure to English outside its study as a subject in its own right, the size of class, availability of books, teaching aids, etc.

Like the student the teacher is also a variable factor in the scheme of teaching a second language; skill and personality of the teacher are instrumental in creating the necessary conditions for learning. Teacher should have proficiency in the language, knowledge in subject matter and expertise in methods and techniques of language teaching which are of reasonable standard. As Robert Lado (1957) says "The language teacher must be educated, at least to the levels of her/his peers. S/he must have the general preparation of a teacher... S/he must know the target language well enough to be imitated by her/his students." The teacher's language is the principal model for the student. In India the main problem is to have competent teachers of English.

English Language Teaching at Cross Roads

The falling standard of English in India is a matter of serious concern for all. There is mushrooming of educational institutions at all levels during the last five decades and this is being done at the expense of quality. It is ironical that with the enormous growth of educational institutions, the achievement of our learners in English is steadily falling. In the past when the grammar translation method was the only method of teaching English, our educational institutions produced very eminent speakers and writers in our country. Many of the old teachers and enlightened persons look back to their own schools days and say that the abolition of grammar is directly responsible for the fall of standards in English. They argue that the translation enabled the learners to have a firm grasp over the meaning of the words and sentences they learnt. They also feel that the replacement of the old grammar translation method by the modern methods/approaches is responsible for the poor quality of teaching English in our country.

The mastery over English which the elders achieved in the past was not due to grammar translation method alone but due to their intensive as well as extensive exposure towards the English language. English was the only medium of instruction then, and the amount of English the learners received and produced was far more than that is attained today, when regional language is the medium of instruction. To come anywhere near the standard of the past any method that is used in the classroom should first of all promote contact frequency.

The Present Scenario

It is very sad to see the way English is being taught and learnt in our schools and colleges, especially in rural areas. A majority of students in rural areas do not have interest to learn English. The foremost reason is the negative attitude and deep-rooted inhibitions against using English for practice in daily life.

Sangeeta and Surender, S. Dhillon (2004) have given a crystal clear picture of the present scenario in English Language Teaching in rural areas: challenges and solutions. The conventional and faulty methods of teaching English being used by untrained and incompetent teachers destroy the natural potential of the learner and the learner may develop hatred towards English. If the learner loses interest in learning English, then, learning process becomes a tedious and nightmarish experience both for the learner and as well as to the teacher. The teacher will be forced to give up the efforts and adopt a casual approach to the business of teaching. In fact one of the biggest challenges before a teacher of English working in rural areas is to create and sustain the interest of the students in English language. Otherwise, it would not be teaching them English; but rather imposing it upon them.

The rural students do not have sufficient proficiency in English at the time of their entry into the college. Hence, they find it difficult to cope up with the advance level of courses of English prescribed by the university. This is the crux of the problem for the college teachers. The tragedy is that even the best teachers fail in the class for no fault. The teacher cannot successfully teach an advanced course of English grammar or English literature to a crowd of students who are not acquainted with the very basics of English. Extremely poor students on one hand and the high level university curriculum on the other hand make the task difficult for the teacher. The job of teaching and learning English becomes a dangerous tight rope-walk, in which both the teachers as well as the learners are but bound to face problems.

Language is basically a tool to understand and conceptualize the universe around and share that understanding with fellow human beings. Therefore, a better understanding of the universe in terms of one's mother tongue will enable one to understand it in terms of a foreign language more easily. A low level of this understanding among the rural area students poses an additional difficulty for them. Poor development of linguistic abilities among rural students is another factor that causes comparatively more difficulties for them in learning a foreign language like English.

P. Gurrey (1966) observes, "The teaching of the mother tongue and the teaching of a foreign language can support and assist each other" because an adult learner of a second language always tries to filter his learning of the new language through the knowledge of his mother tongue. The upshot of the argument is that since rural area students are poor students in their mother tongue they also prove to be poor students of English.

The teacher generally makes use of a combination of the lecture method and grammar translation method in different proportions according to the need and teaches English strictly from the examination point of view. There would be nothing wrong with this if the examination pattern is such that it would assess how far the examinee has been able to acquire the basic linguistic skills in English, namely the ability to listen, speak with correct pronunciation, read and write. But, the examination system only seeks to assess two skills – that of writing and cramming. The examination system is no more a means to assess the real attainments of students; it has rather become an end in itself. To manage a pass in an examination has become the sole aim of students and the teacher's duty is to facilitate it for them. Efficiency in basic linguistic skills is not a part of the examination and it is not made a part of the teaching process. Hence, the basic linguistic skills are ignored.

It is quite common for a learner to commit errors while learning a language. One does it also when one learns one's mother tongue as a child. The learner, therefore, must be encouraged to make maximum use of English even if it is at the cost of accuracy. Accurate use of language is certainly the ideal to be aspired for but to enforce it rigidly from the very early stages of learning would discourage the learner. It is the flow and fluency that needs to be encouraged rather than the accuracy.

To improve the standard of English language teaching efforts may be made from the school level itself. Teaching a foreign language is a highly technical job that requires special skills, which a teacher can learn only through proper training. It is a pity that this fact has not been adequately recognized.

That is why no formal training or degree in the particular field of English teaching is required of a person in order to be eligible for the post of a teacher of English. Ironically enough, it is generally the Social Science teachers in our schools who are teaching English.

It is true that an English teacher alone can't bring about any qualitative change in the scenario of English language teaching in rural areas, unless the systematic loop holes are plugged. However, the teacher will also have to fine tune the methodology to prove as a more vital catalyst in the process of teaching and learning of English. An English teacher at the college level will have to be innovative in the method of teaching. The use of mother tongue may surely be done in the class but only in a very selective and judicious manner. Similarly, the traditional lecture method also needs to be discarded in favor of the Communicative approach to language teaching. This will change the highly teacher oriented teaching process of today to the student oriented one. Language is basically a behavior, which can't be learnt other than through practice. So, the students should be made to play an active role in the learning process. The students must be exposed to English language in its actual use rather than make them cram grammatical rules in isolation. English should be taught as a language and not as an abstract science. Since rural students get no opportunity in the domestic environment to be exposed to English language in a live situation, they must be provided with this kind of opportunity in the classroom. The teacher can do this partly in making maximum use of English in the class. This poses a difficulty in the beginning in the form of resistance by students but proves very effective in the long run.

The teacher-taught ratio must be rationalized. The number of periods allotted to a class must be increased so that the teacher has enough time at disposal to expose the students to the Spoken English and also make them practice it in the class in experimental, imaginative, creative and innovative ways. Since the main problem with rural students is that they do not get enough exposure to English language and due of which they find English language so alien to their sensibility. The teacher will have to simulate such an environment in the class-room for the benefit of the students at least for an hour in a day and devote time to drill work.

Teachers working in rural areas must make careful efforts to relate the process of English teaching to the rural context of the students. The examples, illustrations, models and exercises must be based on the life in the rural set-up. In this regard, it may be stated that preparation of suitable reading material and changes in the courses and syllabi with more emphasis on teaching of English language rather than the classics of English literature. It is high time that the rural students realize the importance of learning English and make sincere efforts to improve their communicative skills in English so as to compete with the urban students.

The Present Attempt

In the first chapter, the investigator presented a broad view of the research study. The significance of language, language skills, importance of learning English, English for communication, glory of English in India, the factors which affect English language learning and the present scenario of English language teaching have been discussed in detail.

The observations in the present study made in foregoing pages demand an in-depth study of the deficiencies/lapses, hurdles/difficulties, conflict between theory and practice in the existing system of English language teaching to make it more effective and purposeful in accordance to the demands of time.

The investigator collected all the relevant literature available in the area of error analysis in English language and research studies in this field, to get sufficient insight for suggesting remedial measures to overcome the deficiencies in the present system to meet the present needs of the society. Further, the investigator has been interested to procure empirical evidence on the basis of the data obtained from all those who are involved in the process of English language teaching namely student trainees to analyze whether their views are in line with the insights obtained by the researcher. The investigator found it worthwhile to conduct an experiment in order to find out whether the errors in writing English language among B.Ed., trainees could be improved by taking up a remedial program. Hence, the present study is *"Error analysis and Remedial program for improving the Writing skills of B.Ed., trainees in English language"*.

Conclusion

To have a conceptual clarity of the subject matter of the current study, an intensive review of related literature has been undertaken in Chapter Two, entitled "Review of Related Literature". The research problem has been stated with its objectives and hypotheses in Chapter Three. Methods employed in the selection of the sample, construction of the tools, collection of data, statistical techniques used in the analysis have been presented in Chapter Four. The analysis of the data and discussion there on are depicted in Chapter Five. The major findings, conclusions arrived at, implications of the study and suggestions for further research have been presented in Chapter Six.

2

A Review of Related Literature

INTRODUCTION

In a review, the researcher "re-views" the "related views" already established by other researchers in the same area in which the study is being undertaken. The literature review demonstrates how the current study advances, refines what already exists. In other words, it indicates the lacunae in the existing knowledge to avoid duplication and monotony. The relevant studies have been critically reviewed and reported. In short, this review is a valuable guide for defining the problem, significance, context of the study, for suggesting appropriate design, data gathering devices and sources of data. It is a logical rationale for formulating the research hypotheses under a wider framework of knowledge. Thus, a review of related literature provides a conceptual framework of reference for the contemplated research and suggests methods, procedures, and sources of data and statistical techniques appropriate for the solutions of the problem.

In the present study, the researcher has made use of related books, periodicals, abstracts, encyclopedias, dissertations, hand books, year books and journals in order to understand the problem and prepare the research design. The literature related to the various components of the present problem involved in the experiment i.e. Error analysis in English has been extensively surveyed.

The review of literature has been divided in to the following categories:

1. Historical background of Error analysis.
2. A Review of Related Research Studies.

Historical Background of Error Analysis

Error analysis, a branch of applied linguistics, emerged in the sixties to demonstrate that learner errors were not only because of the learner's native language but also they reflected some universal learning strategies, as a reaction to contrastive analysis theory, which considered language transfer as the basic process of second language learning as what behaviorist theory suggested. Error analysis deals with the learners' performance in terms of the cognitive processes they make use of in recognizing or coding the input they receive from the target language. Therefore, a primary focus of error analysis is on the evidence that learners' errors provide with an understanding of the underlying process of second language acquisition. At this point, Keshavarz (1997) suggests that the field of error analysis can be divided into two branches: (i) theoretical, and (ii) applied.

Theoretical analysis of errors primarily is concerned with the process and strategies of language learning and its similarities with first language acquisition. In other words, it tries to investigate what is going on in the minds of language learners. Secondly, it tries to decode the strategies of learners such as overgeneralization and simplification, and thirdly, to go to a conclusion that regards the universals of language learning process whether there is an internal syllabus for learning a second language.

Applied error analysis is concerned with organizing remedial courses, and devising appropriate materials and teaching strategies based on the findings of theoretical error analysis.

Identification of Errors

Identifying an error goes beyond explaining what an error is. However, as linguists pay attention to the distinction between an error and mistake, it is necessary to go over the definition of the two different phenomena.

According to Dictionary of Language Teaching and Applied Linguistics (1992) a learner makes a mistake when writing or speaking because of lack of attention, fatigue, carelessness, or some other aspects of performance. Mistakes can be self-corrected when attention is called. Whereas, an error is the use of linguistic item in a way that a fluent or native speaker of the language regards it as showing faulty, incomplete learning. In other words, it occurs because the learner does not know what is correct, and thus it cannot be self-corrected.

To distinguish between an error and mistake, Ellis (1997) suggests two ways. The first one is to check the consistency of learner's performance. If she sometimes uses the correct form and sometimes the wrong one, it is a mistake. However, if she always uses it incorrectly, it is then an error. The second way is to ask learner to try to correct her own deviant utterance. Where she is unable to, the deviations are errors; where she is successful, they are mistakes.

Description of Errors

Corder (1973) classified the errors in terms of the difference between the learners' utterance and the reconstructed version. In this way, errors fall into four categories: Omission of some required element; addition of some unnecessary or incorrect element; selection of an incorrect element; and mis ordering of the elements. He adds that this classification is not enough to describe errors and includes the linguistic level of the errors under the sub-areas of morphology, syntax, and lexicon.

Ellis (1997) has pointed that "classifying errors in this way can help us to diagnose learners' learning problems at any stage of their development and to plot how changes in error patterns occur over time." This categorization can be exemplified as follows:

Omission:

Morphological omission

*A strange thing happen to me yesterday

Syntactical omission	*	Must say also the names?

Addition:

In morphology	*	The pens is here.
In syntax	*	The New York
In lexicon	*	I stayed there during ten years ago

Selection:

In morphology	*	My friend is oldest than me
In syntax	*	I want that she comes here

Ordering:

In pronunciation	*	fignisicant for 'significant';
	*	prulal for 'plural'
In morphology	*	get upping for 'getting up'
In syntax	*	She is a dear to me friend.
In lexicon	*	key car for 'car key'

An error may vary in magnitude. It can include a phoneme, a morpheme, a word, a sentence or even a paragraph. Due to this fact, errors may also be viewed as being either global or local (cited in Brown, 2000). Global errors hinder communication. They prevent the message from being comprehended as in the example below:

- I like bus but my dad tell so not that we must be late for function.

On the other hand, local errors do not prevent the message from being understood because there is usually a minor violation of one segment of a sentence that allows the hearer to guess the intended meaning as follows:

- If I hear from her, I should let you know.

The final group is the two related dimensions of error, domain and extent. Domain is the rank of linguistic unit from phoneme to discourse that must be taken as context in order to understand the error. Extent is the rank of linguistic unit that would have to be deleted, replaced, supplied or recorded in order to repair the sentence. This suggestion by Lennon (cited in Brown, 2000) is parallel with Corder's other categorization of overtly and covertly (1973). Overt errors are unquestionably ungrammatical at the sentence level and covert errors are grammatically well-formed at the sentence level but are not interpretable within the context of communication. For example, "I'm fine, thanks" is a correct sentence but if it is given as answer to the question of "How old are you?" it is covertly error.

Sources of Errors

It has been indicated that errors were assumed as being the only result of interference of the first language habits to the learning of second language. However, with the field of error analysis, it has been understood that the nature of errors implicates the existence of other reasons for errors to occur. Then, the sources of errors can be categorized within two domains: (i) interlingual transfer, and (ii) intralingual transfer.

Interlingual Transfer

Interlingual transfer is a significant source for language learners. Dictionary of Language Teaching and Applied Linguistics (1992) defines interlingual errors as being the result of language transfer, which is caused by the learner's first language. However, this should not be confused with behaviorist approach of language transfer. Error analysis does not regard them as the persistence of old habits, but rather as signs that the learner is internalizing and investigating the system of the new language.

Interlingual errors may occur at different levels such as transfer of phonological, morphological, grammatical and lexica-semantic elements of the native language into the target language. At phonological level, the sounds that cause the students to mispronounce some sounds. They attempt to pronounce '*th*' of 'thank you' as't' of 'tea'; or '*th*' of 'they' as 'd' of 'dean'. Learners tend to place a vowel as in the example of * 'sitation', instead of 'station'. At morphological level, students tend to omit the plural suffix at the end of the word. For example,

- three book
- three student is coming.

Intralingual Transfer

Interferences from the students' own language is not the only reason for committing errors. As Ellis (1997) states, some errors seem to be universal, reflecting learners' attempts to make the task of learning and using the target language simpler. Use of past tense suffix '-ed' for all verbs is an example of simplification and over generalization. These errors are common in the speech of second language learners, irrespective of their mother tongue.

Intralingual errors result from faulty or partial learning of the target language rather than language transfer. They may be caused by the influence of one target language item upon another. For example, learners attempt to use two tense markers at the same time in one sentence since they have not mastered the language yet. When they say: * "He is comes here", it is because the singularity of the third person requires "is" in present continuous, and "-s" at the end of a verb in simple present tense. In short, intralingual errors occur as a result of learners' attempt to build up concepts and hypotheses about the target language from their limited experience with it. Learners may commit errors due to this reason in many ways as in the following examples:

- She made me **to** smile.
- I want **learning** English.
- The fruit smells fresh**ly**.
- Doctors always **gives** us good advices.
- I don't know why **did** he go.

Review of Related Research Studies

There are many studies on error analysis because error analysis helps to improve the teaching and learning process. If learners' errors and the causes of those errors are identified, errors can be corrected, though not all. Moreover, error analysis helps direct the focus of the teaching and learning process. The investigator came across a few doctoral theses by the scholars who have worked on error analysis. They have been presented below in the chronological order in both the Western and Indian contexts.

Review of Related Literature in the Western Context

Angwatankul (1980) conducted a research study on the "Relationship between Communicative competence and learning achievement in English language". He found that most of the errors committed by Thai learners were verb forms, articles and prepositions.

Corder (1981) in his book "Error analysis and Interlanguage" differentiated errors from mistakes in the way that errors are systematic in nature being "errors of competence" which occur in the continuum of the learning process. They are the result of the learners' transitional competence. On the other hand, mistakes are "errors of performance" which are not systematic.

Cumming and *Mellow* (1996) in their research study "An Investigation into the validity of written indicators of second language Proficiency" studied errors at the grammatical morpheme level and found that they can indicate second language learning ability.

Dulay, Burt & Krashen (1982) in their work "Language Two" said the result of error analysis can be used as an indicator of learning achievement and guidance for teaching. One of the difficulties of error analysis is how to define and scope the 'errors' as there are many definitions of errors. *Duskova* (1969) also supported the same idea that learners who avoid using certain structures and have no errors in those errors may not know how to use those structures in his article "One source of errors in foreign language learning."

Edge (1989) in his book "Mistakes and Corrections" defined errors as forms that language users cannot correct by themselves even though they have been taught.

James (1998) in his study "Errors in language learning and use: Exploring error analysis" added that language learners cannot correct their errors until they have additional knowledge on the topic. These errors occur in the course of the learner's study because they haven't acquired enough knowledge. Once they acquire additional knowledge, they will be able to correct their errors and the more errors the learners correct the more conscious of language they will become.

Kitao and *Kitao* (1997) suggested that error analysis in language use can predict the learners' type of errors which will be useful for developing teaching materials and selecting teaching methods in their study "Selecting and developing teaching/learning materials." Moreover, the result of such analysis can be used for researching language acquisition and learners' strategy in language learning.

Michaeldes (1990) in his article "Error analysis: An aid to teaching" analyzed and categorized errors into eight domains according to importance and frequency, such as wrong order of words, wrong tense, wrong use of articles and prepositions.

Newmark and *Reibel* (1968) proposed another approach to ignorance hypothesis which emphasizes avoidance strategy in their article "Necessity and Sufficiency in language learning."

Paster (1986) in his study "The Ilokano ESL learner: A study of inter language" found that most common interlingual errors are using the present simple tense in the place of the past simple tense, using the wrong verb from after modal, no inversion of auxiliary verb in questions, and using the wrong subject verb agreement.

Polio (1997) studied second language writing, and error free writing, the use of the holistic scale, T-units and numbers of errors as criteria and found that counting error numbers may be better for homogenous population in his research work "Measures of linguistic accuracy in second language writing research."

Rujikaitakumjorn and *Chiewkul* (1989) analyzed errors of students at Khon Kaen University and found frequent errors made by students from each faculty and discovered that there is a dependency between errors and each faculty in their study "Error analysis of English language Performance of Khon Kaen University fresh students."

Review of Related Literature in the Indian Context

Abdul Nasir (1997) conducted a study on "Analysis of errors committed by the primary school children in speaking Malayalam Language". The study revealed that the children with severe language disabilities and children with mild language disabilities have difficulties in the following components of language like language (receptive) scores, language (expressive) scores, semantic scores (receptive, expressive) and syntax (receptive, expressive) scores.

Baskaran, Herbart, S. (1989), did an investigation on "The impact of the Remedial teaching programs on the Errors committed by the students of standard XII in written English". The major findings were:

1. The students of the control group did not differ significantly with the experimental group in committing orthographical errors in written English in the pre test.
2. The students of the control group did not significantly differ with the control group in committing orthographical errors in written English in the post test.

Bhaskar (1962) conducted a study on "Analysis of Common Errors in PUC Entrants". The errors committed by PUC students in English were in verb form, reported speech, articles, prepositions and spelling and the study was confined only to collection of errors.

Bindu (1996) analyzed "Reading and Writing errors in Malayalam language among Primary school children". She has analyzed the different types of errors like word substitution errors, letter substitution errors, substitution errors, blending errors and reversal errors in Malayalam language

Chandra Joice, G. (1988), administered a study on "Correlates of Written English at the +2 stage". The major findings were:

1. Proficiency in written English at +2 level was significantly correlated with knowledge of grammar, reading comprehension, vocabulary, the ability to predict lexical and syntactical items and proficiency relationship in Tamil, positive attitude towards English, occupational status of the parents, economic status of the family, reading habits, writing practice and the use of English outside the formal education setting.

2. Proficiency in written English at the +2 level was significantly correlated with the occupational status of parents, economic status of the family and the educational qualifications of the members of the family – it was not school, nor was the subject of specialization, but related to the medium of instruction. English medium pupils scored higher than the Tamil medium pupils.
3. Proficiency in English was related to all the factors in learning habits covering reading habits, writing practice and use of English outside the formal educational setting. There existed a significant relationship between pupil's perception of their performance and their proficiency in written English.

Dave, R.H. and *Saha, S.N.* (1980) carried out a research study on the "Analysis of common errors in English at the Higher Secondary level". The important findings were: errors of grammatical structures were predominantly pronounced, spelling errors were the next most prominent, errors in usage and idioms are also noted.

Devaki, L and *Ramaswamy* (1990), analyzed "Cognitive styles and Errors in Second language Learning". The major findings were:

1. The higher the degree of Field Independence (FI) the lower was the tendency to make global errors and vice versa.
2. The higher the degree of FI the lower was the tendency to over or under generalize the reverse was also true.
3. Low level of FI seemed to be sufficient for identification and use of embedded clauses.
4. Higher level of FI was directly related to ambiguity recognition and level of FI to ambiguity non-recognition.
5. The higher the level of FI the lower was the progress to interference. The lower the level of FI the greater were prone to errors.

Joshi (1975) conducted "A study of errors in written English among pupils of standards V to VII". The study found that typical errors committed by pupils in written English and causes to commit typical errors.

Joshi, V.G. (1985) did the research investigation on "A study of errors in written English and remedial program". The major finding was that the number and quality of errors were reduced after the introduction of the remedial program which included correction of spelling, syntax, written expression and drilling.

Leelavathi (1986) conducted "A study to find out common errors in writing in Kannada class IV students in selected schools in Mysore city and to explore their relationships to some of the personal variables of children". The major findings of the study were:

1. It was found that children belonging to family with lower income levels or lower educational status were poorer in language ability.
2. It also revealed that there is no difference between Kannada and non-Kannada students in acquiring ability in the main language studied in school.

Mohammed T.K. (1986) conducted "A Diagnostic study of errors in written English of Pre Degree students". The findings of the study were:

1. The major errors in written English of Pre degree students were identified.
2. The errors were classified into major functional and grammatical areas.
3. The relative proportion of errors was classified with a view to arrange them into the major areas in the order of their importance.
4. The sources or causes of the errors were identified and
5. Corrective measures through a remedial program have been suggested.

Nair (1986) conducted "A study of common language difficulties of secondary school pupils in Kerala" and analyzed the common language difficulties faced by secondary school pupils in Kerala.

Prameela (1996) carried out "A study on the errors in written Hindi, of the fourth standard students of northern Kerala" and found that majority of the students made mistakes in the area of spelling, rural students made more mistakes in the mechanics of writing and there is not much difference between percentage of urban and rural students, who have committed errors.

Rama (1985) administered a study on "Reading errors in Kannada language among Dyslexia children. She used a Kannada recognition test for children of third and fourth standards. The test included 100 words consisting of almost all the letters of Kannada alphabets and sample of 'kagunitha'. She identified errors among the children while reading word substitution errors, sound blending errors, addition or omission of sounds and reversal errors.

Sarma, Madan Mohan, (1991) did an investigation on the "Errors in written English of Assamese learners at Hr. Sec. Level". The major findings were:

1. About 73.1% of the sentences written by the learners contained one or more errors. Most frequent errors occurred in the following areas: verbs, tenses, passives, articles and prepositions.
2. About 79% of the errors emerged as serious in word order, S-V concord, verbs, lexical items, sequence of tenses, prepositions, articles and negative focus Yes – No questions.

3. The following areas of English grammar were more difficult for Assamese learners: article 'the', prepositions, S-V concord, negative questions, and sequence of tenses, relative clauses and conditional clauses.
4. The strategies adopted by learners generally included differentiation, simplification (semantic and syntactic) over generalization, categorization and extension, translation transfer and communicative strategies or paraphrasing and circumlocution.
5. Only 39.7% of the errors could be traced to a single source. The major sources of errors are: language transfer (25%), ignorance of L2 rules, false assumptions about L2, ignorance of rule restrictions, teaching-learning situation.
6. Transfer errors were more frequent at the syntactic level. Such errors were not necessarily more frequent in the L2 production of the rural students.

Shaikh, A.G. (1992), did "A critical study of errors in Marathi writing committed by Urdu speaking pupils of standard VII". The major findings were:

1. The Urdu pupils found it difficult to write and speak the Marathi language.
2. In Urdu schools English was given more importance than Marathi.
3. The experimental teaching organized for the study was successful in reading the errors.

Sharma, Prasanta, (1989), conducted "A study on the progress of writing abilities with the help of creativity and intelligence of the students". The major findings were:

1. Urban students showed better results in WAT in Bengali than their rural counterparts while the boys and girls, the rural and urban differences did not exist.
2. Urban boys performed better than rural boys and the same was true with urban girls as compared to rural girls.
3. It was found that there existed a +ve correlation between WAT and GI, WAT and Originality; WAT and creativity, WAT fluency and flexibility.
4. WAT scores could be predicted by General Intelligence (GI), originality, fluency and flexibility scores.
5. It was possible to extract a general factor in dimensions identified in writing ability.

Viswesvaraiah and *Vedamani* (1963), in the research study, "A study of the Common Errors in Spelling" found that the errors committed by girls were significantly less than that committed by boys.

Conclusion

This chapter has been devoted to make a survey of the available literature related to Error analysis in English. The literature enabled the researcher to get a right perspective of the theoretical framework. An over view of the studies mentioned above by and large reveals that a few studies have been taken up in the field of Error analysis in English. Therefore the investigator realized the need to conduct the present investigation. The review helped in framing the objectives, and hypotheses of the study. It helped immensely in choosing the variables of the study. The method of investigation was designed based on the light thrown by related studies.

The investigator is aware that the present review is neither exhaustive nor extensive. It has given a synoptic view of the research in error analysis in English.

On the basis of the conclusions and the insights accrued through review of related literature, the research problem with its significance, objectives of the study, hypotheses and variables have been stated in the next chapter.

3

Statement of the Problem and Hypotheses

INTRODUCTION

The investigator has stated the research problem of study, its need, objectives of the study, hypotheses and variables clearly.

Need for the Study

The National Policy on Education (1986) has commented on the sad state of affairs: "Today, a preponderant percentage of students who leave the portals of schools, colleges and universities lack communication skills. They can neither speak nor write fluently". Students in schools, colleges and universities are not receiving adequate training in oral and writing skills. Schools and colleges are neglecting this vital area of education and sending ill-equipped products. Hence, the teachers who are the powerful instruments should bring about reforms in the field of education and mould the future citizens based on the needs. In other words, the students need to be trained to speak and write well by their teachers.

The present standard of teaching of English prevailing in schools and colleges is so poor leading to large number of failures in English at the school and college levels. English is learnt as a second language by the student. In this situation the learner comes in contact with the target language more in its written form. This is true in situations where students learn English in order to gain access to information published in English. Most of the students are not able to rise to the level of use English as a library language, in other words teachers are unable to fulfill the goals of teaching English at the school and college level. Majority of the students even after completing their secondary school education struggle hard to find right expression in their spoken or written form of communication. Often they have ideas, which cannot be translated into proper word constructions. This is not only true of a foreign language, but also of their mother tongue. The most pressing duty of the teacher is to help her students to develop an effective link between her thoughts and words. Very often ideas exist in an amorphous state, vague, undefined, and mixed with ideas that are clearly expressible. The teacher should help the students to search for the dormant ideas which strive hard to assume some recognizable shape. Given a specific situation, the mind of the student wanders into areas where she vaguely sees unrecognized and unidentified links in thought, while the teacher should provide sufficient help to get the main ideas to find expression on paper. She should also help her to explore those regions where material for coherence and logical development of thought exist and give them a concrete shape. Then, it will make any writing readable. But, this is a major problem of most of the students, because the skill of writing is the most difficult and a neglected skill in schools and colleges.

Writing is cognitively a very complex activity as it involves discovering ideas, discovering how to organize them, discovering what one wants to put across to one's readers, achieving success in the use of complex features in the target language such as linkers, for example demands an intensely systematic teaching procedure.

Writing should aim at clear efficient communication. The emphasis should be on communication of ideas. It means that focus is on sequencing and linking of ideas and sentences rather than on grammar. Coherence or clarity of ideas and their cohesion or linkage is what is important. Cohesion is achieved linguistically with linkers or connectives whereas coherence is the way ideas hang together only through linguistic devices, but essentially through an expression of clarity that exists in thinking. Both fluency and accuracy are important in writing. This means to know what to say and to write accurately are important. So, good writing is an expression of clear thinking. This involves many sub skills to make a piece of writing coherent, effective and communicative.

Writing which is an important language skill has to be given due importance. Writing well in any language is a difficult art and needs a great deal of practice. Moreover, the motivation to write in any language is often absent. This is so in a second language like English. Writing adequately in a second language is a painful experience both for teachers and students. The teaching of writing for teachers' particularly continuous writing is a formidable task and to write a sustained piece of writing is a frightening experience for a student. Writing is a complex affair with many sub skills and a neglected skill in an educational program.

It is inevitable that learners make mistakes and commit errors while writing in English. The process can be impeded through realizing the errors and operating on them according to the feedbacks given. The steps that learners follow make the researchers and language teachers realize that if the mistakes and errors of learners in constructing the new language system are analyzed carefully, the process of language acquisition shall be understood.

The analysis of error thus has become a field of linguistics in that sense. The field of language teaching benefit from the findings of linguistics in many cases including error analysis. What a linguist is looking for understanding the language learning process contribute a lot to the questions of language teachers. Many of the teachers complain that their students are unable to use the linguistic forms that they are taught. Lengo (1995) states "this situation is due to the teacher's false impression that output should be an authentic representation of input." This belief ignores the function of intake- that knowledge of language the students internalize. Intake may be different from the teacher's syllabus being subject to be internalized.

Error analysis enables teachers to find out the sources of errors and take pedagogical precautions towards them. Thus, the analysis of learner language has become an essential need to overcome some questions and propose solutions regarding different aspects.

The investigator being a teacher educator in Methods of teaching English found it worthwhile to undertake a research study to identify the errors of B.Ed., trainees while writing in English and suggested a remedial program to overcome errors and improve their writing skills in English. This study is concerned with the error analysis and its contribution to English language teaching at both linguistic and methodological levels.

The investigator has been obsessed with some of the puzzling queries which were the concerns of the study. They have prompted the investigator to undertake this study.

1. What are the common errors committed by B.Ed., trainees while writing in English?
2. What could be the reasons for the B.Ed. trainees to commit errors while writing in English?
3. What measures could be taken to overcome errors while writing in English among B.Ed. trainees?
4. What strategy could be used to improve the writing skills in English among B.Ed., trainees?

Statement of the Problem

The present study is titled as:

"Error Analysis and Remedial program for improving the Writing skills of B.Ed., trainees in English Language"

Objectives

The project has been designed with the following objectives:

1. To identify the errors of B.Ed., trainees in English while writing;

2. To find out the reasons those contribute to errors in English while writing English among B.Ed trainees;
3. To design a remedial program to overcome errors and improve the writing skills of B.Ed. trainees in English language;
4. To study the impact of remedial program to overcome errors and improve the writing skills of B.Ed., trainees in English language;
5. To study the difference between the Pre test score and Post test score for the variable, namely, social status of the family;
6. To study the difference between the Pre test score and Post test score for the selected personal variable, namely, gender;
7. To study the difference between the Pre test score and Post test score for the subject variable, namely, Mathematics, Physical Science, Biological Science and Social Studies among the B.Ed., trainees in English language.

Hypotheses

To realize the above objectives, the following hypotheses have been formulated in null form:

1. There exists no significant difference among the errors committed in English while writing between male trainees and female trainees.
2. There exists no significant association between the reasons those contribute to errors and the errors committed in English while writing among B.Ed trainees.
3. There exists no significant difference in the errors committed in English while writing among B.Ed. trainees before and after the remedial program.
4. There exists no significant difference in the errors committed in English while writing among B.Ed. trainees based on the subjects, namely, Mathematics, Physical Science, Bio-Science and Social Studies either in Pre test or in the Post test of the remedial program.
5. There exists no significant association between the errors committed in English while writing among B.Ed. trainees and the selected family related variable, namely, social status of the family.
6. There exists no significant association between the errors committed in English while writing among B.Ed., trainees and the selected personal variable, namely, gender.

Variables

The following dependent and independent variables have been selected to be included in the project:

Dependent variable: Writing skills in English language is the dependent variable.

Independent variable: Social status of the family and personal variable, namely, gender and subject of specialization has been selected as independent variables in this project.

Operational definitions of Key Terms

Error Analysis: Error analysis is the study of systematic errors in the performance of second language learners. It is a branch of applied linguistics. It is concerned with the compilation, study and analysis of errors made by second language learners and tries to find out the aspects involved in second language acquisition.

Writing skills: It is one of the basic skills of language (L, S, R, W). It is a productive skill. Writing refers to the form of written communication in English.

Writing tasks: Writing tasks are a number of pieces of work to be done by the students to acquire proficiency in the language.

Remedial program: It is a training program or intervention program provided for students with learning difficulties.

B.Ed trainees: Students of Bachelor of Education.

ESL learners: Indian students learn English as a Second Language. Hence, the students are called ESL learners.

Conclusion

The research problem, objectives, hypotheses, variables of the study and operational definitions of the key terms has been stated in this chapter. The method of investigation has been dealt in the subsequent chapter.

4

Methodology

INTRODUCTION

Well planned and properly executed research study produces satisfactory and valid results. The accuracy of the results depends on adoption of appropriate procedures, development and administration of valid tools to collect relevant data and analysis of data by appropriate statistical techniques. In the light of aforesaid cannons, the current chapter entitled "Methodology" discusses the methodological procedure followed in the investigation.

Method of Investigation

Experimental method of investigation is employed in the present study. The research study is conducted in three phases. In the first phase, the errors committed by the B.Ed., trainees in English while writing have been identified. In the second phase, a remedial program based on the errors committed by the B.Ed., trainees in English while writing has been designed. In the third phase, the remedial program has been implemented and finally, the improvement after conducting the experiment has been tested.

Sampling Technique

Purposive sampling technique has been used in the selection of the sample.

Sample of the Study

The sample constituted 100 B.Ed., trainees who opted different optional at B.Ed., level in the School of Education and HRD, Dravidian University.

Design of the Study

The study is carried out in three phases:

Phase 1: ***Test in Writing***

A test in writing has been conducted among B.Ed. trainees to identify the different kinds of errors committed such as in grammar, vocabulary, spelling, punctuation and paragraph writing.

Construction of the Test in Writing

In the construction of the test in writing the different aspects that were kept in mind were:

Importance of English

Importance of English is increasing in the present global world. There is an urgent need for the students to equip themselves with the communication skills in English.

Objectives of Teaching English in B.Ed Course

The objectives of teaching English in the B.Ed course were examined. The experts in the area of educational research, educational administration, curriculum designers and the authors of the textbooks were also consulted.

Identification of the Important Components to be included for the Test in Writing

The following components were considered to be included in this test. They are:

(a) Grammar;

(b) Vocabulary;

(c) Spelling;

(d) Punctuation; and

(e) Paragraph writing.

Selection of items for each Component

Due weightage was given for each component and a good number of items were collected from different sources of research studies. The items thus selected were organized logically in a preliminary form of the test. They were presented before a panel of experts which consisted of English teachers, educationists, researchers and language experts. The panel was asked to scrutinize the items and comment critically on the adequacy and the accuracy of the items. The suggestions given by the panel were taken into consideration and the items were modified and refined accordingly.

Pilot Study

A Pilot study was conducted in the test in writing. The students were asked to answer all the items without imposing any time limit to complete the test.

Item Analysis

In the present study, the answer scripts of the pilot sample were scored according to the scoring key prepared in the test construction. Based on the total score obtained by each student, the answer scripts were arranged in the ascending order. 27% of the top group and 27% of the bottom group scripts were selected and the remaining scripts were discarded.

Examining each item in the lower group as well as the higher group, the marks obtained by each student for each question item were posted. The difference between the scores of the higher and lower groups indicated the discrimination power of the item. The discrimination power and difficulty value of each item was calculated. Items possessing reasonable difficulty value and good discrimination power were retained for the final form of the test.

Table 4.1: Details of the Items in Test in Writing based on Components

S. No.	Name of the Component	Marks	No. of items (Qs) given	Question Numbers
1.	Grammar	12	22	1-22
2.	Vocabulary	3	3	23-25
3.	Spelling	2	2	26-27
4.	Punctuation	2	1	28
5.	Paragraph Writing	6	1	29
	Total	25 marks	29 questions	

Table 4.1 shows the details of the items in test in writing based on the components. The final form of the test in writing has 29 items and the maximum marks were 25. The question numbers have also been indicated. (The final form of the "Test in Writing" is shown in the Appendix-2.)

Scoring Key

The scoring key was prepared for valuing the test and the manuscripts were valued.

Validity of the Test

Content Validity

The final form of the test was presented to a panel of experts which consisted of English teachers, educationists, researchers and language experts for scrutiny. They were requested to examine the coverage of the content in the test items keeping in view the objectives of teaching English in B.Ed course and also the future needs of the student. They expressed their satisfaction regarding the coverage of the important components in the test. The experts also accepted the weightage given for each component as shown in the final form of the test.

Construct Validity

While constructing the test, the scientific procedure of construction of a test was meticulously followed in each and every step. The experts examined the percentages given for each item and distribution of items in the test. The item analysis procedure followed while selecting the test items and the table of components in the final form reveals that the test possesses construct validity.

Reliability of the Test

Test-retest method was adopted to determine the reliability of the test. The final form of the test was administered to a representative sample of students at the first instance and the same test was administered to the same group of students after a gap of 4 weeks. The scores obtained in the first trial were compared with the scores obtained in the second trial. The high correlation revealed that the test is reliable (r = 0.750).

Phase 2: *Preparation of Writing Package*

The errors committed by B.Ed. trainees in writing English language have been identified in phase 1 by conducting the Pre test. The errors which were 50% and above were considered as contents to be included in the writing package based on the percentage of errors in the pre test score. The investigator prepared the writing package/instructional material to implement the remedial program. The writing package has been designed to help B.Ed. trainees overcome the errors and improve their writing skills in English language.

Writing Package

The writing package has been organized on the following sub heads:

I. Grammar

1. Tenses
2. Subject Verb Agreement
3. Conditional Sentences.
4. Modal Auxiliary
5. Passive Voice
6. Degrees of Comparison
7. Reported Speech
8. Kinds of Sentences
9. Simple, Complex and Compound Sentences
10. Relative Pronouns and Clauses
11. Articles
12. Prepositions

II. Vocabulary

III. Spelling

IV. Punctuation

V. Paragraph Writing

With the preparation of the writing package the objective, *"to design a remedial program to overcome errors and improve the writing skills in English among B.Ed. trainees"* has been realized. (Final form of the "Writing package" is shown in the Appendix- 1).

Phase 3: ***Experimentation***

The remedial program has been taken up for the B.Ed. trainees in the School of Education and HRD, Dravidian University, Kuppam. The experimental sample consisted of 100 B.Ed., trainees who opted different optional such as Mathematics, Physical Science, Bio Science and Social Studies. A test in writing in English has been administered and the pretest scores were tabulated. The errors identified were of 25 kinds and they carried 25 points. The kinds of errors were:

1. Use of Noun
2. Use of Verb
3. Use of Adjective
4. Use of Adverb
5. Use of Pronoun
6. Use of Article
7. Use of Preposition
8. Use of Gerund
9. Choice of Vocabulary
10. Subject Verb Agreement
11. Use of Tenses
12. Use of Conditional
13. Passive Voice
14. Reported Speech
15. Relative Pronouns and Clauses
16. Degrees of Comparison
17. Punctuation
18. Spelling
19. Kinds of Sentences
20. Simple, Complex & Compound sentences

21. Use of Modal
22. Topic Sentence
23. Unity
24. Coherence
25. Cohesion

The errors which were 50% and above in the pre test score were considered as contents to be included in the writing package.

Table 4.2: Pre test: Frequency of Errors in Percentages

Order	Kinds of Errors	Frequency of Errors in Percentages
1.a	Cohesion	100%
1.b	Coherence	100%
1.c	Unity	99%
2.a	Topic Sentence	99%
2.b	Use of Modal	99%
2.c	Simple, complex & compound sentences	99%
3	Kinds of sentences	90%
4	Spelling	84%
5	Reported speech	80%
6.a	Passive voice	77%
6.b	Use of Conditional	77%
6.c	Use of Tense	77%
7.a	Punctuation	76%
7.b	Degrees of comparison	76%
8	Subject-verb agreement	73%
9	Relative pronouns & clauses	71%
10	Choice of vocabulary	60%
11	Use of Articles	52%
12	Use of Prepositions	50%
13	Use of Gerund	44%
14	Use of Noun	21%
15	Use of Adverb	16%
16	Use of Pronoun	15%
17	Use of Verb	14%
18	Use of Adjective	10%

The writing package has been designed and remedial program implemented to overcome the errors and improve the writing skills in English language among B.Ed., trainees. The remedial program has been planned for one month. The investigator handled about 26 hours on all working days in a month. The students were oriented on each and every content aspect in the writing package. Then, the students were asked to work out the exercises. It has been ensured that all the content aspects were taught with the same zeal and commitment. Practice tests were conducted at the end of each and every week. A post test has been administered at the end of the remedial program to measure whether the B.Ed. trainees could overcome errors and improve their writing skills in English language or not.

Design of the Experiment

The Pre test Post test design has been used to conduct the experiment.

Data Gathering Devices

The Pre test and Post test scores on the test in writing in English have been the data gathering devices. A logical association between the remedial program and observed respondent effects has been attempted.

Scoring of Data

The wrong and right responses obtained by the student in the opinion writing test in English were converted into numerical scores in both the pre test and post test.

Analysis of Data

The data collected using the pre test and post test design was statistically analyzed using the following techniques: percentages, mean, standard deviation, χ^2, 't' test and ANOVA. The difference between Pre test and Post test scores of B.Ed. trainees has been analyzed. The analysis revealed that there has been improvement between the pre test scores and post test scores. The difference has been tested for significance by applying 't' test at 0.01 level of confidence. The mean differences have been tested for significance by applying analysis of variance (ANOVA) at 0.01 level of confidence. The significant results show that the remedial program has been effective to overcome errors and improve the writing skills in English language among B.Ed. trainees.

Conclusion

The detailed analysis of the data and discussion of the results has been presented in the succeeding chapter.

5

Discussion and Results

INTRODUCTION

This chapter attempts to present the data and analyze the data with the help of suitable statistical techniques. Further, the interpretation of data has led to draw the findings, conclusions, educational implications and recommendations for further research.

Use of Noun **Table 5.1**

	Pre test	Post test	Total
Wrong Answers	21	4	25
	21.00	4.00	12.50
Right Answers	79	96	175
	79.00	96.00	87.50
Total	100 100.00	100 100.00	200 100.00
			χ^2 – 13.2111**

The observation of the table 5.1 reveals that the critical value of χ^2 13.2111** is significant at 0.01 level of confidence. It indicates that the remedial program is effective to overcome errors in writing English as there is improvement in the post test score in terms of use of Noun.

Use of Verb **Table 5.2**

	Pre test	Post test	Total
Wrong Answers	14	2	16
	14.00	2.00	8.00
Right Answers	86	98	184
	86.00	98.00	92.00
Total	100 100.00	100 100.00	200 100.00
			χ^2– 9.783**

Table 5.2 reveals that the critical value of χ^2 9.783** which is significant at 0.01 level of confidence. This shows that there is improvement in the post test score in terms of use of Verb. It is quite evident that the remedial program is effective to overcome errors in writing English language among B.Ed., trainees.

Use of Adjective **Table 5.3**

	Pre test	Post test	Total
Wrong Answers	10	0	10
	10.00	0.00	5.00
Right Answers	90	100	190
	90.00	100.00	95.00
Total	100 100.00	100 100.00	200 100.00
			χ^2– 10.526**

From table 5.3, it is seen that the χ^2 value 10.526** is significant at 0.01 level of confidence. This indicates that the remedial program is effective to overcome errors and improve their writing skills in English language from the post test score in terms of use of Adjective.

Use of Adverb **Table 5.4**

	Pre test	Post test	Total
Wrong Answers	16	1	17
	16.00	1.00	8.50
Right Answers	84	99	183
	84.00	99.00	91.50
Total	100 100.00	100 100.00	200 100.00
			χ^2– 14.465**

It is evident from table 5.4, that the χ^2 critical value 14.465** is significant at 0.01 level of confidence. There is improvement in the post test score in terms of use of Adverb which indicates that the remedial program is effective to overcome errors in writing English language among B.Ed. trainees.

Use of Pronoun **Table 5.5**

	Pre test	Post test	Total
Wrong Answers	15	3	18
	15.00	3.00	9.00
Right Answers	85	97	182
	85.00	97.00	91.00
Total	100 100.00	100 100.00	200 100.00
			χ^2– 8.791**

Table 5.5 indicates that the value of χ^2 8.791** which is significant at 0.01 level of confidence. It indicates that the remedial program is effective to overcome errors in writing English language among B.Ed. trainees. This also shows that there is improvement in post test score in terms of use of Pronoun.

Use of Article

Table 5.6

	Pre test	Post test	Total
Wrong Answers	52	29	81
	52.00	29.00	40.50
Right Answers	48	71	119
	48	71	119
Total	100 100.00	100 100.00	200 100.00
			χ^2– 10.976**

It is observed from table 5.6, that the χ^2 value 10.976 is significant at 0.01 level of confidence. There is improvement in the post test score in terms of use of articles which reveals that the remedial program is effective to overcome errors in writing English language.

Use of Preposition

Table 5.7

	Pre test	Post test	Total
Wrong Answers	50	31	81
	50.00	31.00	40.50
Right Answers	50	69	119
	50.00	69.00	59.50
Total	100 100.00	100 100.00	200 100.00
			χ^2– 7.490**

It is seen from table 5.7, that the χ^2 value 7.490** is significant at 0.01 level of confidence. This shows that there is improvement in the post test score in terms of use of Prepositions which indicates that the remedial program is effective to overcome errors in writing English language.

Choice of Vocabulary

Table 5.8

	Pre test	Post test	Total
Wrong Answers	60	37	97
	60.00	37.00	48.50
Right Answers	40	63	103
	40.00	63.00	51.50
Total	100 100.00	100 100.00	200 100.00
			χ^2– 10.590**

The observation of the table 5.8 reveals that the critical value of χ^2 10.590** is significant at 0.01 level of confidence. It indicates that the remedial program is effective to overcome errors in writing English as there is improvement in the post test score in terms of choice of Vocabulary.

Use of Gerund

Table 5.9

	Pre test	Post test	Total
Wrong Answers	44	3	47
	4400	3.00	23.50
Right Answers	56	97	153
	56.00	97.00	76.50
Total	100 100.00	100 100.00	200 100.00
			χ^2– 46.753**

It is evident from table 5.9, that the χ^2 critical value 46.753** is significant at 0.01 level of confidence. There is improvement in the post test score in terms of use of Gerund which indicates that the remedial program is effective to overcome errors in writing English language among B.Ed. trainees.

Subject Verb Agreement

Table 5.10

	Pre test	Post test	Total
Wrong Answers	73	35	108
	73.00	35.00	54.00
Right Answers	27	65	92
	27.00	65.00	46.00
Total	100 100.00	100 100.00	200 100.00
			χ^2– 29.066**

From table 5.10, it is seen that the χ^2 value 29.066** is significant at 0.01 level of confidence. This indicates that the remedial program is effective to overcome errors and improve their writing skills in English language from the post test score in terms of use of Subject Verb Agreement.

Use of Tense

Table 5.11

	Pre test	Post test	Total
Wrong Answers	77	9	86
	77.00	9.00	43.00
Right Answers	23	91	114
	23.00	91.00	57.00
Total	100 100.00	100 100.00	200 100.00
			χ^2– 94.329**

It is observed from table 5.11, that the χ^2 value 94.329** is significant at 0.01 level of confidence. There is improvement in the post test score in terms of use of Tenses which reveals that the remedial program is effective to overcome errors in writing English language.

Use of Conditionals **Table 5.12**

	Pre test	Post test	Total
Wrong Answers	77	5	82
	77.00	5.00	41.00
Right Answers	23	95	118
	23.00	95.00	59.00
Total	100 100.00	100 100.00	200 100.00
			χ^2– 107.152**

Table 5.12 indicates that the value of χ^2 107.152** which is significant at 0.01 level of confidence. It indicates that the remedial program is effective to overcome errors in writing English language among B.Ed. trainees. This also shows that there is improvement in post test score in terms of use of Conditionals.

Passive Voice **Table 5.13**

	Pre test	Post test	Total
Wrong Answers	77	2	79
	77.00	2.00	39.50
Right Answers	23	98	121
	23.00	98.00	60.50
Total	100 100.00	100 100.00	200 100.00
			χ^2– 46.753**

From table 5.13, it is seen that the χ^2 value 46.753** is significant at 0.01 level of confidence. This indicates that the remedial program is effective to overcome errors and improve their writing skills in English language from the post test score in terms of use of Passive Voice.

Reported Speech **Table 5.14**

	Pre test	Post test	Total
Wrong Answers	80	10	90
	80.00	10.00	45.00
Right Answers	20	90	110
	20.00	90.00	55.00
Total	100 100.00	100 100.00	200 100.00
			χ^2– 98.990**

It is evident from table 5.14, that the χ^2 critical value 98.990** is significant at 0.01 level of confidence. There is improvement in the post test score in terms of use of Reported Speech which indicates that the remedial program is effective to overcome errors in writing English language among B.Ed. trainees.

Relative Pronouns and Clauses

Table 5.15

	Pre test	Post test	Total
Wrong Answers	71	3	74
	71.00	3.00	37.00
Right Answers	29	97	126
	29.00	97.00	63.00
Total	100 100.00	100 100.00	200 100.00
			χ^2– 99.185**

Table 5.15 indicates that the value of χ^2 99.185** which is significant at 0.01 level of confidence. It indicates that the remedial program is effective to overcome errors in writing English language among B.Ed. trainees. This also shows that there is improvement in post test score in terms of use of Relative Pronouns and Clauses.

Degrees of Comparison

Table 5.16

	Pre test	Post test	Total
Wrong Answers	76	2	78
	76.00	2.00	39.00
Right Answers	24	98	122
	24.00	98.00	61.00
Total	100 100.00	100 100.00	200 100.00
			χ^2– 115.090**

It is observed from table 5.16, that the χ^2 value 115.090** is significant at 0.01 level of confidence. There is improvement in the post test score in terms of use of Degrees of Comparison which reveals that the remedial program is effective to overcome errors in writing English language.

Punctuation

Table 5.17

	Pre test	Post test	Total
Wrong Answers	76	24	100
	76.00	24.00	50.00
Right Answers	24	76	100
	24.00	76.00	50.00
Total	100 100.00	100 100.00	200 100.00
			χ^2– 54.080**

It is seen from table 5.17, that the χ^2 value 54.080** is significant at 0.01 level of confidence. This shows that there is improvement in the post test score in terms of use of Punctuation which indicates that the remedial program is effective to overcome errors in writing English language.

Spelling

Table 5.18

	Pre test	Post test	Total
Wrong Answers	84	19	103
	84.00	19.00	51.50
Right Answers	16	81	97
	16.00	81.00	48.50
Total	100 100.00	100 100.00	200 100.00
			χ^2– 84.576**

The observation of the table 5.18 reveals that the critical value of χ^2 84.576** is significant at 0.01 level of confidence. It indicates that the remedial program is effective to overcome errors in writing English as there is improvement in the post test score in terms of use of Spelling.

Kinds of Sentences

Table 5.19

	Pre test	Post test	Total
Wrong Answers	90	8	98
	90.00	8.00	49.00
Right Answers	10	92	102
	10.00	92.00	51.00
Total	100 100.00	100 100.00	200 100.00
			χ^2– 134.534**

It is evident from table 5.19, that the χ^2 critical value 134.534** is significant at 0.01 level of confidence. There is improvement in the post test score in terms of use of Kinds of Sentences which indicates that the remedial program is effective to overcome errors in writing English language among B.Ed. trainees.

Simple, Complex and Compound Sentences

Table 5.20

	Pre test	Post test	Total
Wrong Answers	99	19	118
	99.00	19.00	59.00
Right Answers	1	81	82
	1.00	81.00	41.00
Total	100 100.00	100 100.00	200 100.00
			χ^2– 132.286**

From table 5.20, it is seen that the χ^2 value 132.286** is significant at 0.01 level of confidence. This indicates that the remedial program is effective to overcome errors and improve their writing skills in English language from the post test score in terms of use of Simple, Complex and Compound sentences.

Modals

Table 5.21

	Pre test	Post test	Total
Wrong Answers	99	37	136
	99.00	37.00	68.00
Right Answers	1	63	64
	1.00	63.00	32.00
Total	100 100.00	100 100.00	200 100.00
			χ^2– 88.327**

Table 5.21 reveals that the critical value of χ^2 is 88.327** which is significant at 0.01 level of confidence. This shows that there is improvement in the post test score in terms of use of Modals. It is quite evident that the remedial program is effective to overcome errors in writing English language among B.Ed., trainees.

Topic Sentence

Table 5.22

	Pre test	Post test	Total
Wrong Answers	99	8	107
	99.00	8.00	53.50
Right Answers	1	92	93
	1.00	92.00	46.50
Total	100 100.00	100 100.00	200 100.00
			χ^2– 166.436**

Table 5.22 indicates that the value of χ^2 166.436** which is significant at 0.01 level of confidence. It indicates that the remedial program is effective to overcome errors in writing English language among B.Ed. trainees. This also shows that there is improvement in post test score in terms of use of Topic sentence.

Unity

Table 5.23

	Pre test	Post test	Total
Wrong Answers	100	30	130
	100.00	30.00	65.00
Right Answers	0	70	70
	0.00	70.00	35.00
Total	100 100.00	100 100.00	200 100.00
			χ^2– 107.692**

The observation of the table 5.23 reveals that the critical value of χ^2 107.692** is significant at 0.01 level of confidence. It indicates that the remedial program is effective to overcome errors in writing English as there is improvement in the post test score in terms of use of Unity.

Coherence

Table 5.24

	Pre test	Post test	Total
Wrong Answers	100	32	132
	100.00	32.00	66.00
Right Answers	0	68	68
	0.00	68.00	34.00
Total	100 100.00	100 100.00	200 100.00
			χ^2– 103.030**

It is observed from table 5.24, that the χ^2 value 103.030** is significant at 0.01 level of confidence. There is improvement in the post test score in terms of use of Coherence which reveals that the remedial program is effective to overcome errors in writing English language.

Cohesion

Table 5.25

	Pre test	Post test	Total
Wrong Answers	100	42	142
	100.00	42.00	71.00
Right Answers	0	58	58
	0.00	58.00	29.00
Total	100 100.00	100 100.00	200 100.00
			χ^2– 81.690**

It is evident from table 5.25, that the χ^2 critical value 81.690** is significant at 0.01 level of confidence. There is improvement in the post test score in terms of use of Cohesion which indicates that the remedial program is effective to overcome errors in writing English language among B.Ed. trainees.

The null hypothesis formulated for all the tables from 5.1 to 5.25, *"there exists no significant difference in the errors committed in English while writing among B.Ed. trainees even after the remedial program"* is not accepted. Thus, the objective, *"to study the impact of remedial program to overcome errors and improve the writing skills of B.Ed. trainees in English language"* is achieved.

ANOVA for Pre test Score

Mean differences in the Scores Among the Subjects Variable based on Pre test Score

The following tables show the distribution of scores on Pre test for the Subjects variable and the differences among them.

Table 5.26: Distribution of scores on Pre test for the Subjects variable

Subjects	N	Mean	SD
Mathematics	30	15.03	6.58
Physical science	15	8.93	4.97
Biological science	24	16.21	6.52
Social Studies	31	17.19	7.23

The mean value of 30 Mathematics students is 15.03 with a SD of 6.58. The mean value of 15 Physical Science students of is 8.93 with a SD of 4.97. The mean value of 24 Biological Science students of is 16.21 with a SD of 6.52. The mean value of 31 Social Studies students of is 17.19 with a SD of 7.23.

The mean differences have been tested for significance by applying Analysis of Variance (ANOVA). The following table shows the values.

Table 5.27: Analysis of Variance for the Mean Difference of Scores on Pre test Score for the Subjects Variable

Source	*df*	SS	MSS	F-ratio
Bet. Groups	3	735.811	245.270	5.465**
Wit. Groups	96	4308.699	44.882	

The 'F' ratio (5.465**) at 0.01 level of confidence from the table reveals that there is significant difference among the four subjects namely, Mathematics, Physical Science, Biological Science and Social studies students in their pretest score. Hence, the null hypothesis formulated, *"there exists no significant difference in the errors committed in English while writing among the B.Ed., trainees based on the subjects, namely, Mathematics, Physical Science, Biological Science and Social Studies"* is not accepted. Thus, the objective, *"to study the association between the pre test score and the subjects' variable, namely, Mathematics, Physical Science, Biological Science and Social Studies"* is achieved.

The following tables show the distribution of scores on Pre test score for the social status of the family.

Table 5.28: Association between Social Status of the Family and Pre test Score

Social Status	N	Mean	SD
OC	23	14.57	7.95
BC	48	15.42	6.84
SC	21	15.67	7.18
ST	8	12.88	5.06

The mean value of 23 OC students is 14.57 with a SD of 7.95. The mean value of 28 BC students is 15.42 with a SD of 6.84. The mean value of 21 SC students is 15.67 with a SD of 7.18. The mean value of 8 ST students is 12.88 with a SD of 5.06.

The mean differences have been tested for significance by applying analysis of variance (ANOVA). The following table shows the values.

Table 5.29: Analysis of Variance for the Mean Difference of Scores on Pre test Score for the Social Status of the Family

Source	*df*	SS	MSS	F-ratio
Bet. Groups	3	57.648	19.216	0.370ns
Wit. Groups	96	4986.861	51.946	

The 'F' ratio (0.370ns) is not significant and reveals that there is no significant difference among the four social groups viz. OC, BC SC and ST students in their pre-test score.

Thus, the null hypothesis formulated that, *"there exists no significant association between the pre-test score and the social status of the family"* is accepted. From the above analysis of the pre-test score of the students the objective *"to study the association between the pre-test score and the social status of the family"* included in this study is realized.

ANOVA for Post Test Score

Mean Differences in the Scores among the Subjects Variable based on Post test Score

The following tables show the distribution of scores on Post test for the Subjects variable and the differences among them.

Table 5.30: Distribution of Scores on Post test for the Subjects Variable

Subjects	N	Mean	SD
Mathematics	30	30.60	2.87
Physical science	15	30.80	3.71
Biological science	24	30.08	2.75
Social Studies	31	29.16	2.62

The mean value of 30 Mathematics students is 30.60 with a SD of 2.87. The mean value of 15 Physical Science students is 30.80 with a SD of 3.71. The mean value of 24 Biological Science students is 30.08 with a SD of 2.75. The mean value of 31 Social Studies students is 29.16 with a SD of 2.62.

The mean differences have been tested for significance by applying Analysis of Variance (ANOVA). The following table shows the values.

Table 5.31: Analysis of Variance for the Mean Difference of Scores on Post test Score for the Subjects Variable

Source	df	SS	MSS	F-ratio
Bet. Groups	3	42.008	14.003	1.586ns
Wit. Groups	96	847.633	8.830	

The 'F' ratio (1.586 ns) is not significant and reveals that there is no significant difference among the four subjects viz., Mathematics, Physical Science, Biological Science and Social Studies students in their post-test score.

Thus, the null hypothesis formulated that, *"there exists no significant difference in the errors committed in writing English language among the B.Ed. trainees based on the subjects, namely, Mathematics, Physical Science, Biological Science and Social Studies"* is accepted. From the above analysis of the Post test score of students the objective *"to study the association between the post test score and the Subjects variables, namely Mathematics, Physical Science, Biological Science and Social Studies"* is realized.

The following tables show the distribution of scores on post test score for the social status of the family.

Table 5.32: Association between Social Status of the Family and Post test Score

Social Status	N	Mean	SD
OC	23	31.83	2.30
BC	48	30.00	2.69
SC	21	29.43	2.74
ST	8	27.00	3.67

The mean value of 23 OC students is 31.83 with a SD of 2.30. The mean value of 48 BC students is 30.00 with a SD of 2.69. The mean value of 21 SC students is 29.43 with a SD of 2.74. The mean of 8 ST students is 27.00 with a SD of 3.67.

The mean differences have been tested for significance by applying Analysis of Variance (ANOVA). The following table shows the values.

Table 5.33: Analysis of Variance for the Mean Difference of Scores on Post test Score for the Social Status of the Family

Source	*df*	SS	MSS	F-ratio
Bet. Groups	3	155.195	51.732	6.762**
Wit. Groups	96	734.445	7.650	

The 'F' ratio (6.762**) is significant at 0.01 level of confidence and reveals that there is a significant difference among the four social groups viz., OC, BC, SC and ST students in their post test score.

Thus, the null hypothesis formulated that, *"there exists no significant association between the post test score and the social status of the family"* is not accepted. From the above analysis of the post test score of the students the objective, *"to study the association between the post test score and the social status of the family"* included in this study is realized.

Table 5.34: Difference of Means between Pre test and Post test on the Variable Test in Writing

Test inWriting	Pre test			Post test			t-value
	N	Mean	SD	N	Mean	SD	
Right answers	100	15.070	7.102	100	30.060	2.983	19.459**
Wrong Answers	100	19.930	7.102	100	4.940	2.983	

** = Significant at 0.01 level, * = Significant at 0.05 level & ns = Not Significant

The mean score of the right answers is 15.070 with a SD of 7.102 in the pre test and the mean score of the right answers is 30.060 with a SD of 2.983 in the post test. It is tested for significance by applying 't' test. The 't' value is 19.459** which is significant at 0.01 level of confidence. This reveals that the students have improved their writing skills in English language after the remedial program. Based on this the null hypothesis formulated, *"there exists no significant difference in the errors committed by B.Ed., trainees in English while writing even after the remedial program"* is not accepted.

The mean score of the wrong answers is 19.930 with a SD of 7.102 in the pre test and the mean score of the wrong answers is 4.940 with a SD of 2.983 in the post test. It is tested for significance by applying't' test. The't' value is 19.459 which is significant at 0.01 level of confidence. This reveals that the students have overcome their errors after the remedial program and hence there has been improvement in their writing skills in English language among B.Ed., trainees. Based on this the null hypothesis formulated, *"there exists no significant difference in errors committed by B.Ed trainees in English while writing even after the remedial program"* is not accepted.

Table 5.35: Difference of Means between Male Trainees and Female Trainees on Pre test Score and Post test Score

Gender	Pre test			Post test			t-value
	N	Mean	SD	N	Mean	SD	
Males	67	14.418	7.029	67	29.716	3.041	16.351**
Females	33	16.394	7.067	33	30.758	2.731	10.892**

** = Significant at 0.01 level, * = Significant at 0.05 level & ns = Not Significant

The Pre test mean score of 67 male trainees is 14.418 with a SD of 7.029 and the post test mean score is 29.716 with a SD of 3.041. It is tested for significance by applying't' test. The't' test value is 16.357** which is significant at 0.01 level of confidence. The Pre test mean score of 33 female trainees is 16.394 with a SD of 7.067 and the Post test mean score is 30.758 with a SD of 2.731. The 't' test value is 10.892** which is significant at 0.01 level of confidence. This reveals that the male and female trainees could overcome the errors and improve their writing skills in English language after the remedial program. Based on this, the null hypothesis, *"there exists no significant difference in the errors committed in English while writing between male trainees and female trainees"* is not accepted.

Table 5.36: Difference of Means between Pre test and Post test Scores on the Variable – Subjects

Subjects	Pre test			Post test			t-value
	N	Mean	SD	N	Mean	SD	
Mathematics	30	15.033	6.580	30	30.600	2.871	11.877**
Physical Science	15	8.933	4.973	15	30.800	3.709	13.651**
Biological Science	24	16.208	6.519	24	30.083	2.753	9.606**
Social Studies	31	17.194	7.226	31	29.161	2.616	8.670**

** = Significant at 0.01 level, * = Significant at 0.05 level & ns = Not Significant

The pre test mean score of 30 Mathematics trainees is 15.033 with a SD of 6.580 and the post test mean score is 30.600 with a SD of 2.871. The't' value is 11.877** which is significant at 0.01 level of confidence. The pre test mean score of 15 Physical Science trainees is 8.933 with a SD of 4.973 and the post test mean score is 30.800 with a SD of 3.709. The't' value is 13.651** which is significant at 0.01 level of confidence. The pre test mean score of 24 Biological Science trainees is 16.208 with a SD of 6.519 and the post test mean score is 30.083 with a SD of 2.753. The't' value is 9.606** which is significant at 0.01 level of confidence. The pre test mean score of 31 Social Studies trainees is 17.194 with a SD of 7.226 and the post test mean score is 29.161 with a SD of 2.616. The 't' value is 8.670** which is significant at 0.01 level of confidence. All the above obtained values reveal that the Mathematics trainees, Physical

Science trainees, Biological Science trainees and Social Studies trainees could overcome errors and improve their writing skills in English language after the remedial program.

The null hypothesis formulated, *"there exists no significant difference in the errors committed by B.Ed. trainees in English while writing based on the subjects', namely, Mathematics, Physical Science, Biological Science and Social Studies"* is not accepted.

Table 5.37: Difference of Means between Pre test and Post test Scores on the Variable – Social Status

Social Status	Pre test			Post test			t-value
	N	Mean	SD	N	Mean	SD	
OC	23	14.565	7.950	23	31.826	2.297	10.004**
BC	48	15.417	6.840	48	30.000	2.693	13.745**
SC	21	15.667	7.180	21	29.429	2.736	8.208**
ST	8	12.875	5.061	8	27.000	3.674	6.388**

** = Significant at 0.01 level,* = Significant at 0.05 level & ns = Not Significant

The pre test mean score of 23 OC trainees is 14.565 with a SD of 7.950 and the post test mean score is 31.826 with a SD of 2.297. The 't' value is 10.004** which is significant at 0.01 level of confidence. The pre test mean score of 48 BC trainees is 15.417 with a SD of 6.840 and the post test mean score is 30.000 with a SD of 2.693. The 't' value is 13.745** which is significant at 0.01 level of confidence. The pre test mean score of 21 SC trainees is 15.697 with a SD of 7.180 and the post test mean score is 29.429 with a SD of 2.736. The 't' value is 8.208** which is significant at 0.01 level of confidence. The pre test mean score of 8 ST trainees is 12.875 with a SD of 5.061 and the post test mean score is 27.000 with a SD of 3.674. The 't' value is 6.388** which is significant at 0.01 level of confidence.

It is observed that the OC, BC, SC and ST trainees could overcome errors and improve their writing skills in English language after the remedial program.

The null hypothesis, *"there exists no significant difference in the errors committed in the writing skill of B.Ed. trainees in English language based on the social status of the family"* is not accepted.

Table 5.38: Difference between Frequency of Errors on Pre test Score and Post test Score

Order	Kinds of Errors	Frequency of Errors in Pre test Score	Frequency of Errors in Post test Score	Post test Score
1.a	Cohesion	100%	42%	58%
1.b	Coherence	100%	32%	68%
1.c	Unity	99%	30%	70%
2.a	Topic Sentence	99%	8%	92%
2.b	Use of Modal	99%	37%	63%
2.c	Simple, complex and compound sentences	99%	19%	81%
3	Kinds of sentences	90%	8%	92%
4	Spelling	84%	19%	81%
5	Reported speech	80%	10%	90%
6.a	Passive voice	77%	2%	98%
6.b	Use of Conditional	77%	5%	95%
6.c	Use of Tense	77%	9%	91%
7.a	Punctuation	76%	24%	76%
7.b	Degrees of comparison	76%	2%	98%
8	Subject-verb agreement	73%	35%	65%
9	Relative pronouns & clauses	71%	3%	97%
10	Choice of vocabulary	60%	37%	63%
11	Use of Articles	52%	29%	71%
12	Use of Prepositions	50%	31%	69%
13	Use of Gerund	44%	3%	97%
14	Use of Noun	21%	4%	96%
15	Use of Adverb	16%	1%	99%
16	Use of Pronoun	15%	3%	97%
17	Use of Verb	14%	2%	98%
18	Use of Adjective	10%	Nil	100%

The difference between the pre test and post test scores show that there is remarkable improvement in the post test score among the B.Ed. trainees. It is quite obvious that the writing package that was implemented during the remedial program has been very effective and helpful for the B.Ed. trainees to overcome errors and improve their writing skills in English.

The null hypothesis formulated, *"there exists no significant difference in the errors committed in English while writing among B.Ed., trainees even after the remedial program"* is not accepted. The objective, *"to study the impact of remedial program to overcome errors and improve the writing skills of B.Ed., trainees, in English language"* is realized.

Conclusion

The results and findings of the investigation helped to draw out the conclusions, educational implications and suggestions for further research, which have been presented in the next chapter.

6

Findings, Conclusions Educational Implications and Suggestions for further Research

INTRODUCTION

The findings of the study, conclusions of the study, educational implications and suggestions for further research have been presented in this chapter.

Findings of the Study

The significant findings which emerged in the course of investigation are as follows:

1. It is found that 12 kinds of errors were identified in Pre test score and their frequency was above 50%.
2. None of the trainees had cohesion and coherence in writing a paragraph in the pre test. The frequency of errors has decreased to 42% and 32% respectively in the post test after the intervention program.
3. It is found that 99% of the trainees committed errors in the unity of the paragraph, in writing the topic sentence, use of modal and simple, complex and compound sentences in the pre test. The frequency of errors has reduced to 30%, 8% and 37% respectively in the post test after the intervention program.
4. The frequency of errors of the trainees in the pre test in using different kinds of sentences was 90% and in the post test, the percentage of errors has come down to 8% and this is because of the implementation of the intervention/remedial program.
5. 84% of the trainees have gone wrong in spelling in the pre test. The frequency of errors has reduced to 19% in their post test.
6. 80% of the trainees could not use reported speech correctly in the pre test. The frequency of errors has decreased to 10% in the post test after the intervention program.

7. It is found that 77% of the trainees could not use passive voice, conditionals and tenses in the right manner. The frequency of errors has gone down to 2%, 5% and 9% respectively in the post test and this shows that the remedial program is very effective.
8. In the pre test, 76% of the trainees have not used proper punctuation marks and the degrees of comparison. In the post test, the frequency of errors has reduced to 24% and 2% respectively due to the intervention program.
9. 71% of the sample could not use relative pronouns and clauses properly in their pre test. There is improvement in the post test score and the frequency of errors has decreased to 3% and this is due to the intervention program.
10. It is found that 60% of sample could not use the right word in the right place in the pre test. The frequency of errors in the post test reveals that the errors have decreased to 37% and this improvement is because of the effective remedial program.
11. It is found that 52% of the trainees could not use articles in the pre test. The frequency of errors has reduced to 29% in the post test after the intervention program.
12. 50% of the trainees could not use prepositions in the pre test. Their usage of prepositions has improved in post test and the frequency of errors has decreased to 31% after the intervention program.
13. It is found that the trainees have committed interlingual errors like misuse of modal verbs, misuse of punctuation, misuse of subject-verb agreement and misuse of pronoun at morphological and grammatical levels while writing in English.
14. It is found that the trainees have committed intralingual errors like misuse of tense, misuse of conditionals, misuse of spelling, misuse of relative pronouns, misuse of vocabulary, misuse of articles, misuse of prepositions, misuse of gerund, misuse of nouns, verbs, adverbs and adjectives, errors in change of voice and change of direct speech, errors in transforming kinds of sentences, errors in topic sentence, unity, cohesion and coherence from partial learning of the target language at morphological and grammatical levels while writing in English.
15. It is also found that the trainees have committed more serious errors like fragmented sentences and run-on sentences upon reviewing their manuscripts.
16. There is significant improvement in the Post test score after the remedial program.

17. There is a significant difference in the Pre test score among the four subjects, namely, Mathematics, Physical Science, Biological Science and Social studies.
18. There is no significant association between the social status of the family and the Pre test score.
19. There is significant association between the social status of the family and the Post test score.
20. There is a significant association between the variable gender and Post test score.
21. There is a significant association between the Post test score and the subjects, namely, Mathematics, Physical Science, Biological Science and Social studies.
22. The research finding can be used as criteria for material development in the writing lab. It would enable to isolate the errors the trainees' make. Then, provide proper teaching learning materials and measures to correct their errors. It would help to improve the English ability of prospective teachers to communicate better with few errors.

Conclusions of the Study

From the above findings the following conclusions have been drawn out in the present research study:

1. Majority of the B.Ed., trainees committed different kinds of errors and in most of the cases they were more than 50%. All the trainees are from the rural background and did not have proper exposure towards the English language during their schooling. Moreover, lack of competent English teachers at the school level is one of the reasons that contribute to errors while writing in English language.
2. The remedial program is effective to overcome the errors and improve the writing skills in English among B.Ed., trainees. This is quite evident from the Post test score.
3. The Post test score reveals that the writing package that is designed for implementation in the remedial program has been very effective to overcome errors and improve the writing skills in English among B.Ed., trainees.
4. The trainees exhibited significant improvement in their writing skills and could overcome different kinds of errors like interlingual and intralingual errors after the remedial program.
5. The Post test score indicates that there is no significant difference among the four subjects. It is quite obvious that there is

improvement in the Post test score among all the four subjects, namely, Mathematics, Physical Science, Biological Science and Social studies.

6. There is a significant association between the Post test score and the social status of the family. Higher the status of the family more interest among the trainees to improve their writing skills in English.

Educational Implications

The present project is a significant attempt in the direction of Error analysis in English language teaching and learning. The results and findings would be quite useful for the college teachers of English. Some of the educational implications derived from the findings of the study:

1. The study has revealed the fact that spelling of learners' errors and then, providing instructions can help the students maintain and increase their interest in learning English.
2. The study makes crystal clear that the remedial program is more effective to overcome errors to a maximum extent and improve their writing skills in English.
3. The study reveals that the writing package designed has helped trainees overcome errors to a maximum extent and improve their writing skills in English through remedial program.
4. To develop self instructional material to overcome errors and improve their writing skills in English.
5. The English language teachers are suggested to take steps to diagnose the different kinds of errors (both interlingual and intralingual errors) committed by college students so as to improve the writing skills in English.
6. In service training programs should be organized to improve the standards of teaching English among the existing English teachers at the college level.

Suggestions

1. To equip the trainees with a more efficient approach to writing, a writing lab should be established and efficiently utilized to facilitate and supplement the writing process and assessment. The findings will be useful for providing materials in the writing lab where the prospective teachers can equip themselves with higher language proficiency.
2. In a broader context, the research findings suggest that if student trainees practice frequently, they will eventually be able to write

well in English. If these findings can be generalized, it will greatly benefit the English second language teaching and learning process in the near future.

3. Replication of the study may be done with different samples in other professional courses.

Conclusion

The findings, conclusions, educational implications of the study have been presented in this chapter. Certain aspects for further exploration have also been suggested.

Bibliography

Books Consulted

Bhatia, S.V. (1998). *English Language Teaching Methods and Materials: A Critical Study*. New Delhi: Himanshu Publications.

Brown, H.D. (2000). *Principles of Language Learning and Teaching*. New York, Longman.

Burton, S.H. & Humphries, J.A. (1992). *Mastering English Language*. Palgrave Master Series, Published by Palgrave Macmillan.

Byrne, D. (1986). *Teaching Oral English*. London: Harlow and Longman.

Chomsky, N. (1965). *Aspects of the Theory of Syntax:* Boston: MIT Press.

CIEFL, (2003). *"Course Materials of PGCTE and PGDTE"*, Hyderabad: Published by Central Institute of English and Foreign Language.

Corder, S.P. (1973). *Introducing Applied Linguistics. Harmondsworth*: Penguin.

Corder, S.P.(1987). *Error analysis and Interlanguage*. Oxford, Oxford University Press.

David Cameron (1995). *Mastering Modern English*, New Delhi: Orient Longman Ltd., 1/24, Asaf Ali Road.

Dodson, C.J. (1967). *Language Teaching and the Bilingual Method*. Pitman and Sons.

Dulay, H., Burt, M & Krashen, S.D. (1982). *Language Two*. MA. Rowley: Newbury House.

Duskova, L. (1969). *One Source of Errors in Foreign Language*. IRAL.

Edge, J. (1989). *Mistakes and Correction*. London: Longman.

Ellis, R. (1994). *The Study of Second Language Acquisition*. Oxford: Oxford University Press.

Ellis, R. (1997). *Second Language Acquisition* Oxford: Oxford University Press.

Freeman, S (1986). *Written Communication in English*. Bombay: Orient Longman.

French, F.G. (1972). *Teaching of English as an International Language*. London: Oxford University Press.

Fries, C.C. (1948). *Teaching and Learning Foreign Language.* Michigan: University of Michigan Press.

Geoffrey Broughton. (1980). *Teaching English as a Foreign Language.* Published by Routiedge, New York.

Gokak, V.K. (1964). *English in India – it's Present and Future.* New York: Asia Publishing House.

Gurrey, P. (1966). *Teaching of English as a Foreign Language.* London: Longmans Green and Co.

Jagadisan, S. and Murugaiayan, N. (2003). *Common Errors in English,* Hyderabad: Neelkamal Publications Pvt. Ltd., Sultan Bazar.

James, C. (1998). *Errors in Language Learning and Use:* Exploring Error Analysis. London: Longman.

Jeyaraju, M.A. (1992). *English Proficiency for Indian Students,* Gandhigram: Gandhigram Rural Institute (Deemed University).

Keshavarz, M.H. (1997). *Contrastive Analysis and Error Analysis.* Tehran, Rahmana Pub.

Kohli, A.B, (1989). *Techniques of Teaching English.* New Delhi: Reliance Publishing House.

Krishnaswamy, N. and Sriraman, T. (1994). *English Teaching in India,* Chennai: T.R. Publications, PMG Complex, II Floor 57, South Usban Rd., T. Nagar.

Lado, Robert (1957). *Linguistics Across Cultures. University of Michigan Press ELT, Michigan, USA.*

Lado, Robert (1971). *Language Teaching: A Scientific Approach.* Bombay: Tata McGraw Hill Publishing Co. Ltd.

Lawrence, Shaffer. *Skills in Writing,* (2000). New Delhi: IVY Publishing House, Delhi, Sarup & Sons, 4740/23, Ansari Road, Darya Ganj.

Nagaraj, Geetha. (1989). *English Language Teaching.* Bombay: Orient Longman.

Narayanaswami, V.R. (2001). *Strengthen your Writing,* Chennai: Orient Longman Ltd., 160, Anna Salai.

Pahuja, N.P. (2002). *Teaching of English,* New Delhi: Anmol Publications Pvt. Ltd., 4374/4B, Ansari Rd., Daryaganj.

Paul Verghese, C. (2002). *Teaching English as a Second Language,* New Delhi: Sterling Publishers Pvt. Ltd.

Prabhu, N.S. (1987). *Writing without Teachers.* London: Oxford University Press.

Richards, J.C. (1992). *The Language Teaching Matrixes.* London: Cambridge University Press.

Richards, J.C. (ed.) (1974). *Error Analysis: Perspectives in Second Language Acquisition.* London: Longman.

Richards, J.C. *et al.* (1992). *Dictionary to Language Teaching and Applied Linguistics.* Essex, Longman.

Robertson, D. (2001). *Writing Effectively,* New Delhi: Publisher Sarup & Sons, 4740/23, Ansari Road, Darya Ganj.

Shaik Mowla (2002). *Techniques of Teaching English,* Hyderabad: Neelkamal Publications Pvt. Ltd., Sultan Bazar.

Sharma, R.A. (1999), *Fundamentals of Teaching English,* Meerut: Surya Publications.

Shivendra K. Verma and Hemalatha Nagarajan (1999). *An Interactive Grammar of Modern English,* New Delhi: Frank Bros. & Co. (Publishers) Ltd., 4675-A, Ansari Road, 21 Daryaganj.

Sujatha Mukiri (2003). *Enrich your Communication in English,* Hyderabad: Lorven Publications, 1-9-295/9/3, Vidyanagar.

Ur, P. (1996). *A Course in Language Teaching.* Cambridge, Cambridge University Press.

Articles and Papers Consulted

Bhaskar, A.W.S. (1962). *Analysis of Common Errors in PUC Entrants,* Bulletin of Central Institute of English.

Corder, S.P. (1978). *"Language-Learner"*, Understanding Second and Foreign Language Learning: Issues and Approaches. (Ed.) J. Richards. Rowley Mass: Newbury House.

Dulay, H.C. and Burt, M.K. (1974). *Errors and Strategies in Child's Second Language Acquisition. TESOL Quarterly.*

Hatch, E.R. (1978). *"Acquisition of Syntax in a Second Language", Understanding Second and Foreign Language Learning: Issues and Approaches.* (Ed.) Richards, J., Rowly, Mass: Newbury House.

James, C. (1994). *Don't Shoot my dodo: On the Resilience of Contrastive and Error Analysis.* International Review of Applied Linguistics.

Kitao, K. & Kitao, S. (1997). *Selecting and Developing Teaching/Learning Materials.* http://www.Atech.ac.jp/-iteslj/ Articles/ Kitao-Material.Html. April 20.

Lengo, N. (1995). *What is an Error? English Teaching Forum,* 33(3), 20-24.

Manivannan, G. (2006). *"The Importance of English Language".* Using English.com.

Meryl Thompson (1997). *"Professional Ethics and the Teacher: Towards a General Teaching"* England: Published by Trentham Books, Wales.

Michaeldes N.N. (1990). *Error Analysis: An Aid to Teaching. English Teaching Forum,* 28(4).

National Policy on Education (1986). Document Published by Government of India, Department of Education, Ministry of Human Resource Development, New Delhi.

Newmark, L. & Reibel, D.A. (1968) *Necessity and Sufficiency in Language Learning. IRAL, 6(3).*

Sangeeta and Surender, S. Dillon (2004). *English Language Teaching in Rural areas: Challenges and Solutions,* in Hyderabad: EDUTRACKS, Neelkamal Publications, Sultan Bazar.

Vacide, Erdogan (2005). *Contribution of Error Analysis to Foreign Language Teaching,* Journal of Faculty of Education, Vol. I, Issue. Published by Mersin University.

Vivienne Maddock. (1995). *"Development of Skills", English Language Teaching at Cross Roads.* (Eds.) Gautam Banarjee and Siddhartha Ganguly. Titagarh: Linkman Publications.

Xavier, (1988). *"Innovations in Indian English Language Teaching",* Chennai: Loyala Experiment, Loyala College.

Dissertations Cited

Abdul Nasir (1997). *"Analysis of Errors Committed by the Primary School Children in Speaking Malayalam Language".* Dissertation Submitted to University of Bangalore.

Anchalee Sattayatham and Somchoen Honsa, *"Medical Students' Most Frequent Errors at Mahidol University"* Dissertation Submitted to Mahidol University, Thailand.

Angwatanakul, S. (1980). Relationship between Communicative Competence and Learning Achievement in the English Language. *Chulalonkorn Educational Review,* Chulalongkorn University.

Baskaran, Herbert, S (1989). *The Impact of Remedial Teaching Programs on the Errors Committed by the Students of Standard XII in Written English,* M.Phil in Education Submitted to Alagappa University, Karaikudi, Tamilnadu.

Bhaskar, (1962). *An Analysis of Common Errors in PUC Entrants,* Dissertation Submitted to RIE, Mysore.

Bindu, (1996). *Reading and Writing Errors in Malayalam Language Among Primary School Children,* Dissertation Submitted to University of Bangalore.

Chandra Joice, G. (1988). *"Correlates of Written English at the +2 stage",* Unpublished Ph.D. Thesis Submitted to University of Madras.

Corder, S.P. (1981). *Error Analysis and Interlanguage.* Oxford: Oxford University Press.

Cumming, A., & Mellow, D. (1996). *An Investigation into the Validity of Written Indicators of Second Language Proficiency.* In A. Cumming and R. Berwick (Eds.), *Validation in Language Testing Clevendon:* Multilingual Matters.

Dave, R.H. and Saha, S.N. (1980). *Analysis of Errors in English at the Higher Secondary Level*. Report of the Fifth Conference on Chairman and Secretaries of the Boards of Secondary Education, NCERT, New Delhi.

Devaki, L and Ramaswamy (1990). *"Cognitive Styles and Errors in Second Language Learning"*, Dissertation Submitted to University of Bangalore.

Joshi, (1975). *A Study of Errors in Written English Among Pupils of Standards V to VII,* Dissertation Submitted to University of Bangalore.

Joshi, V.G. (1985). *A Study of Errors in Written English and Remedial Program,* Dissertation Submitted to University of Bangalore.

Leelavathi, M.N. (1986). *A Study to find out Common Errors in Writing Kannada Among IV Class Students in Selected Schools in Mysore City,* M.B. Buch, Third Survey of Research in Education, NCERT, New Delhi.

Mohammed T.K. (1986). *A Diagnostic Study of Errors in Written English of Pre-degree Students,* M.B. Buch. Third Survey of Research in Education, NCERT, New Delhi.

Nair (1986). *A Study of Common Language Difficulties,* M.B. Buch, Third Survey of Research in Education, NCERT, New Delhi.

Pastor, A.C. (1986). *The Ilokano ESL learner: A Study of Interlanguage.* M.A. Thesis: National University of Singapore.

Polio, C.G. (1997). *Measures of Linguistic Accuracy in Second Language Writing Research.* Dissertation Submitted to University of Singapore.

Rujikiatgumjorn, S. and Chiewkul, S. (1989). *Error Analysis of English Language Performance of KKU freshman Students. PASAA.*

Sarma, Madan Mohan (1991). *Errors in Written English of Assamese Learners at Higher Secondary Level,* Unpublished Ph.D. Thesis Submitted to Dibugarh University, Karnataka.

Shaikh, A.G. (1992). *A Critical Study of Errors in Marathi Writing Committed by Urdu Speaking Pupils of Standard VII,* Ph.D. Thesis Submitted to University of Pune.

Sharma, Prasanta (1989). *A Study on the Prognosis of Writing Abilities with the help of Creativity and Intelligence of the Students,* unpublished Ph.D. Thesis Submitted to University of Kalyan.

Visweswaran and Vedamani (1963). *A Study of the Common Errors in Spelling,* M.B. Buch, Second Survey of Research in Education, NCERT, New Delhi.

Appendix-1

Writing Package

Contents

Page Number

1. TENSES

1. The tense of a verb indicates the time in which action occurs/occurred/will occur as well as the degrees of completion of the action.
2. The different times indicated by the tenses of verbs are: Present, Past and Future.
3. Under present, past and future times, four different degrees of completion of the action are indicated by four different forms of the verb: Simple, Progressive, Simple Perfect and Progressive Perfect.

Usage of Tenses

4. The Simple present tense is used to denote:

   1. a fact that exists.

Examples:

(i) Mr. Bharat has two children.

(ii) Roses are beautiful.

   2. a scientific/universal truth.

Examples:

(i) The earth goes round the sun.

(ii) Lazy people hate work.

   3. a habit/custom

Examples:

(i) I usually go to college by bus.

(ii) She eats two times a day.

   4. an action that will take place in the immediate future.

Examples:

(i) I leave for Bangalore tomorrow.

(ii) Ranjita arrives here this evening.

5. An action that is part of a program for the future.

Examples:

(i) She goes to London next year.

(ii) We elect a new Secretary next month.

6. To form the Simple present tense of a verb, the infinitive (the basic form of the verb) is used as it is. However, if the subject of the verb is

in the third person singular, s/es is added to the infinitive. The infinitive *be* becomes *am/is/are,* the choice depending upon the person and the number of the subject.

7. The Progressive present tense is used to denote:

    1. An action that is currently going on.

Examples:

(i) We are learning grammar now.

(ii) She is watching television now.

2. An action that will take place in the immediate future.

Examples:

(i) I am leaving for Bangalore tomorrow.

(ii) She is arriving here this evening.

3. An action that is part of a program for the future.

Examples:

(i) I am leaving for London next year.

(ii) We are electing a new Secretary next month.

8. To form the Present progressive tense of a verb, the – *ing* form of the infinitive, called the participle, is used, preceded by the auxiliary/helping verb *am/is/are,* the choice depending upon the person and the number of the subject.

9. The Simple present perfect tense is used to denote:

    1. An action that has just been completed.

Examples:

(i) She has just now returned from Hyderabad.

(ii) We have just now finished the work.

2. An action that has been completed and is reported without the time being specified.

Examples:

(i) We have seen the Red Fort.

(ii) She has repaid the loan.

10. To form the Simple present perfect tense of a verb, the past participle form of the infinitive given in any standard dictionary, is used, preceded by the auxiliary verb *have/has,* the choice depending upon the person and the number of the subject.

11. The Progressive present perfect tense is used to denote:
    1. an action which began in the past, has been going on till now and is likely to continue in the future.

Examples:

(i) She has been taking this medicine for the past five years.

(ii) We have been learning English grammar for the past ten years.

12. To form the Progressive present perfect tense of a verb, the – *ing* form of the infinitive, called the participle, is used, preceded by the word *been* (the past participle form of *be),* in turn preceded by the auxiliary verb *have/has,* the choice depending upon the person and the number of the subject.
13. The Simple past tense is used to denote:
    1. an action that occurred at a specific point of time in the past (the time is either specified or is understood from the context).

Examples:

(i) Govind retired in 1996.

(ii) Many civilians died in the Gulf war.

14. To form the Simple past tense of a verb, the past tense form of the infinitive given in any standard dictionary, is used.
15. The Progressive past tense is used to denote:
    1. An action that was going on during a specified period of time in the past.

Examples:

(i) I was sleeping from 2 to 6 p.m. yesterday.

(ii) They were travelling round the world from May 15 to June 15 last year.

2. An action of a comparatively long duration which occurred in the past and formed the background to another action in the past (momentary or of comparatively very short duration).

Examples:

(i) While they were working in the garden the phone rang in the hall.

(ii) As he was turning a corner, a lorry knocked him down.

16. To form the Progressive past tense of a verb, the – *ing* form of the infinitive, called the participle, is used, preceded by the auxiliary verb *was I were,* the choice depending upon the person and the number of the subject.

17. The Simple past perfect tense is used to denote:

    (i) an action in the past which was completed before another action in the past occurred.

Examples:

(i) When he reached the station, the train had already left and so he could not attend the interview in Hyderabad.

(ii) After the master had gone to bed, the servants made merry.

18. To form the Simple past perfect tense of a verb, the past participle form of the infinitive, given in any standard dictionary, is used, preceded by the auxiliary verb *had.*

19. The Progressive past perfect tense is used to denote:

    1. one of two actions in the past which began earlier than the other, was comparatively of a long duration and was going on till the moment of occurrence of the other action (momentary or of comparatively very short duration.

Examples:

(i) They had been searching for six hours when they spotted a broken wing of the missing plane.

(ii) She had been acting for ten years when she received the award.

20. To form the Progressive past perfect tense of a verb the - *ing* form of the infinitive, called the participle, is used, preceded by the word *been* (the past participle form of *(be),* in turn preceded by the auxiliary verb *had.*

21 The Simple future tense is used to denote:

    1. an action that will occur at a specified point of time in the future.

Examples:

(i) I shall go to Bangalore next week.

(ii) She will leave for England next month.

22. To form the Simple future tense of a verb, the infinitive is used, preceded by the auxiliary verb *shall/will.*

23. The auxiliary verbs *shall* and *will*/may be used interchangeably. However, it is advisable to use *shall* with subjects in the first person (I and *we)* and *will* with subjects in the second and in third person (*you, he, she, it, Ravi, Meera, they, students).*

24. Futurity can also be denoted by using phrases like *intend to, expect to, am/are/is going to,* followed by an infinitive. In such cases the tense of the verb is determined by its form, though the meaning points to the future.

Examples:

(i) She expects to receive her salary today.

(ii) We intend to start a school soon.

(iii) I am going to apply for that job.

25. The Progressive future tense is used to denote:

 1. An action that will be going on during a specified period of time in the future.

Examples:

(i) I shall be sleeping from 2 to 6 p.m. tomorrow.

(ii) We shall be discussing several problems from sunrise to sunset next sunday.

26. To form the Progressive future tense of a verb, the - *ing* form of the infinitive is used, preceded by *shall be/will be.*

27. The Simple future perfect tense is used to denote:

 (i) An action that will have been completed by a specified point of time in the future.

Examples:

(i) By 2016 we shall have built a house.

(ii) By tomorrow evening I shall have completed this task.

28. To form the Progressive future tense of a verb, the past participle of the infinitive, given in any standard dictionary is used, preceded by *shall have/will have.*

Note:

The deadline (point of time in the future) by which the action will have been completed must be specified.

29. The Progressive future perfect tense is used to denote:

 (i) An action that, at a specified point of time in the future, will have been going on for a specified period of time.

Examples:

(i) In 2016 I shall have been teaching English for twenty years.

(ii) In 2016 she will have been acting for twenty years.

30. To form the Progressive future tense of a verb, the – *ing* form of the infinitive is used, preceded by *shall have been/will have been.*

Note:

The point of time in the future with reference to which the period of duration of the action is calculated must be specified.

Exercise

Use the words given in the brackets and frame sentences in the appropriate tense.

1. The moon (go) round the sun as well as the earth.
2. I (play) for the past four hours.
3. I (go) to college now.
4. He (work) in the rain since this morning.
5. They (wait) for two hours, but the train (not arrive) yet.
6. Generally thieves (not like) honest work.
7. While I (paint) the door I fell down.
8. The Professor (go) out before the boys reached his house.
9. I swam across the lake while it (rain).
10. She remembered that the manager (give) her a holiday.
11. I (fly) from Chennai to Delhi when I heard the news.
12. She (act) for ten years when she won the award.
13. The mail (leave) before I reached the Post Office.
14. My sister (buy) a car next month.
15. By 2020 he (write) ten books.
16. He (complete) the task already.
17. Who (help) you next year?
18. We (enjoy) the party last evening.
19. We never (see) ourselves as others do.
20. Just now I (send) a telegram to you.
21. He (act) for the past ten years.
22. She (succeed) in whatever he attempted.
23. He (teach) since 2000.
24. We (not eat) anything since yesterday.
25. The match (start) before we reached the stadium.
26. Sheetal often (wear) a green sari.

27. He helped me as he (promise).
28. She (know) English better than French.
29. He (work) in a factory for twenty years before he became a politician.
30. He (never climb) a mountain.
31. Someone (steal) my watch.
32. Do not disturb me because I (prepare) for an interview.
33. The postman (bring) a parcel for you yesterday.
34. He was standing on the platform when the two trains (collide).
35. Although I (travel) all my life I have never visited Africa.
36. She (be) to Australia.
37. In 2016 he (work) in this factory for twenty years.
38. By next June I (publish) thirty books.

Scoring key

1. The moon goes round the sun as well as the earth.
2. I played for the past four hours.
3. I will go to college now.
4. He worked in the rain since this morning.
5. They waited for two hours, but the train did not arrive yet.
6. Generally thieves don't like honest work.
7. While I was painting the door I fell down.
8. The Professor went out before the boys reached his house.
9. I swam across the lake while it rained.
10. She remembered that the manager gave her a holiday.
11. I flew from Chennai to Delhi when I heard the news.
12. She acted for ten years when she won the award.
13. The mail left before I reached the Post Office.
14. My sister will buy a car next month.
15. By 2020 he shall have written ten books.
16. He had completed the task already.
17. Who will help you next year?
18. We enjoyed the party last evening.
19. We never see ourselves as others do.

20. Just now I sent a telegram to you.
21. He has been acting for the past ten years.
22. She succeeded in whatever he attempted.
23. He has been teaching since 2000.
24. We did not eat anything since yesterday.
25. The match had started before we reached the stadium.
26. Sheetal often wears a green sari.
27. He helped me as he promised.
28. She knows English better than French.
29. He worked in a factory for twenty years before he became a politician.
30. He never climbed a mountain.
31. Someone has stolen my watch.
32. Do not disturb me because I am preparing for an interview.
33. The postman brought a parcel for you yesterday.
34. He was standing on the platform when the two trains collided.
35. Although I have travelled all my life I have never visited Africa.
36. She has been to Australia.
37. In 2016 he shall have been working in this factory for twenty years.
38. By next June I shall have published thirty books.

2. SUBJECT VERB AGREEMENT

1. The verb of a sentence must always be in agreement with its subject in number and person. Such agreement is known as Concord.
2. If the subject consists of two/more nouns connected by *and,* the verb is plural.

Examples:

(i) Ranjita and Sobhita are coming here today.

(ii) Lata, Monu and Maria have left us.

(iii) Mr. Bharat and his students have arrived.

3. If the subject consists of two/more singular nouns referring to the same person/thing, the verb is singular.

Examples:

(i) My friend and roommate has arrived.

(ii) Your friend, roommate and classmate has left the University.

4. If the subject consists of two/more nouns which together express a single idea, the verb is singular.

Examples:

(i) Rice and sambar is the regular meal of South Indians.

(ii) Bread, butter and jam make a good breakfast.

5. If the subject is preceded by the word *each/every*, the verb is singular.

Examples:

(i) Each student and teacher has to participate in this program.

(ii) Every man, woman and child has to contribute to national development.

6. If the subject consists of two/more nouns of different numbers joined by *or/nor*, the verb is plural and the plural noun is placed next to the verb.

Examples:

(i) Ravi or his sisters are guilty of this.

(ii) Neither he nor they were worried.

(iii) Tom, Harry or their parents have to repay the money.

(iv) Neither John, Paul nor their brothers have arrived.

7. If the subject consists of two/more nouns of different persons joined by *or/nor*, the verb agrees in person with the noun nearest to it.

Examples:

(i) Either you or he has to come.

(ii) Neither he nor I am interested in it.

(iii) Either you, she or I have to do this.

8. If the subject is a collective noun referring to the group as a whole, the verb is singular. But, if the individuals/the components are referred to, the verb is plural.

Examples:

(i) The council has elected him President.

(ii) The committee was divided on the question of an additional tax.

9. If the subject is a noun which is plural in form but singular in meaning, the verb is singular.

Examples:

(i) The news is not quite good.

(ii) Your scissors is with me.

(iii) Your trousers are torn.

10. If the subject is a relative pronoun (*who/that),* the verb agrees in number and person with the antecedent of the relative pronoun (that is, the noun which the relative pronoun replaces).

Examples:

(i) You, who is my best friend, has to help me now.

(ii) Bharat is one of the best actors that have ever lived.

(iii) One of my friends, who lives in America, is coming here today.

11. If the subject is a singular noun to which other singular/plural nouns are joined by words/phrases like *with, together with, as well as, in addition* to etc., the verb is singular.

Examples:

(i) The General, with all his officers, has surrendered to us.

(ii) Ritesh as well as Kiran gets a medal.

(iii) Ravi, not Rohit, is my cousin.

(iv) Kiran, in addition to Ravi, is helping me to do this.

(v) This jewel, together with two houses, has been given to me by my grandmother.

12. If the subject is a phrase like *many a man/many an actor* (which is always plural in meaning), the verb is singular.

Examples:

(i) Many a warrior has died today.

(ii) Many an elephant is killed for its tusk in Africa.

Exercise

Rewrite the following sentences using the words given in brackets.

1. Kiran, like Ravi, is hard-working. (Both Kiran and Ravi).
2. No student likes to write tests. (Few).
3. The black and the white cow are grazing in the field (The black and white cow).
4. The General and his wife belong to Mumbai. (as well as)

5. All citizens have to obey the country's laws. (Every).
6. We have agreed to the proposal. (None)
7. All young men and women have to serve the nation in one way or another. (Each)
8. The students were dismissed. (One of)
9. The students and the teachers are interested in this program. (Neither)
10. Indu and Chandu have to carry out this task. (Either)
11. All of us have to make sacrifices for the nation. (Each one)
12. The Principal and the President of the Association are absent. (The Principal and President of the Association)
13. Politics and the cinema spoil students. (as well as)
14. Ritesh as well as Kiran is a good boy. (Both)
15. Kumar and Ramesh are testing that machine. (in addition to)
16. One student was punished. (A few)
17. They are going to Delhi. (None of)

Scoring Key

1. Both Kiran and Ravi are hard-working.
2. Few students like to write tests.
3. The black and white cow is grazing in the field.
4. The General as well as his wife belong to Mumbai.
5. Every citizen has to obey the country's laws.
6. None agreed to the proposal.
7. One of the students was dismissed.
8. Neither the students nor the teachers are interested in this program.
9. Either Indu and Chandu has to carry out this task.
10. Each one of us has to make sacrifices for the nation.
11. The Principal and the President of the Association were absent.
12. Politics as well as cinema spoil students.
13. Both Ritesh and Kiran are good boys.
14. Ramesh in addition to Kumar is testing that machine.
15. A few students were punished.
16. None of them are going to Delhi.

3. CONDITIONAL SENTENCES

1. Three different types of Conditional sentences are used. Each type has distinct meaning and uses a distinct combination of tenses.

2. **Type (1)**

Example:

(i) *If you work hard you will succeed.*

In this type the condition (*If you work hard)* is expressed in the simple present tense, while the result (*you will succeed)* is expressed in the simple future tense.

In this type the explicit meaning is that, if the specified condition (*if you work hard)* is fulfilled, the specified result (*you will succeed)* will definitely follow. This type also carries the implied meaning that, if the specified condition is not fulfilled, the specified result will definitely not follow. So, the given sentence can also be rewritten, without any change of meaning, to read, *If you do not work hard you will not succeed/Unless, you work hard you will not succeed.*

3. **Type (2)**

Example:

If it rained tomorrow he would cancel the meeting.

In this type the condition (*If it rained tomorrow)* is expressed in the simple past tense, while the result (*he would cancel the meeting)* is expressed in the future past tense. The whole sentence, however, refers to future events only.

In this type relationship between the condition and the result is not quite definite. The given sentence merely means that, if the specified condition (*if it rained tomorrow)* is fulfilled, the specified result (*he would cancel the meeting)* will follow. This sentence cannot be rewritten to read. *If it did not rain tomorrow he would not cancel the meeting.*

4. **Type (3)**

Example

If you had studied well you would have passed.

In this type the condition (*if you had studied well*) is expressed in the Simple past perfect tense, while the result (*you would have passed*) is expressed in the simple future past perfect tense. The whole sentence refers to past events.

In this type the meaning is that the specified condition (*if you had studied well*) was not fulfilled and, therefore, the specified result (*you would have passed*) did not follow. So the given sentence can be rewritten, without any change of meaning. *You did not study well and therefore you did not pass.*

Exercise

Rewrite the following sentences, using the infinitives given within brackets in the appropriate tense.

1. If you start now you (reach) Bangalore by 7 P.M.
2. If the firm (pay) better wages there would be no labour trouble.
3. If you do not win the match we (go) home by the next train.
4. Unless you study sincerely you (not pass).
5. If they had told me the truth I (help) them.
6. If they (start) early they would have caught the train.
7. If you (have) better luck you would have got the job.
8. Unless we have time we (not go) to that temple.
9. If he had not broken his promise I (assist) him.
10. If we win this match the Principal (declare) a holiday.
11. If you do not come in time you (not get) your share.
12. If you had studied in Andhra Loyola College you (meet) my elder brother.
13. She would have become a doctor if she (have) money.
14. If you (be) present at the meeting you would have met him.
15. If they planned their trip better they (save) a good deal of money.

Scoring Key

1. If you start now, you will reach Bangalore by 7 P.M.
2. If the firm pays better wages there would be no labour trouble.
3. If you do not win the match, we will go home by the next train.
4. Unless you study sincerely, you will not pass.
5. If they had told me the truth, I would have helped them.
6. If they started early, they would have caught the train.
7. You would have got the job, if you had better luck.
8. Unless we had time, we would not go to that temple.
9. If he had not broken his promise, I would have assisted him.
10. If we win this match, the Principal would declare a holiday.

11. If you do not come in time, you will not get your share.
12. If you had studied in Andhra Loyola College, you would have met my elder brother.
13. She would have become a doctor if she had money.
14. If you were present at the meeting you would have met him.
15. If they planned their trip better, they would save a good deal of money.

4. MODAL AUXILIARY

1. Sometimes a special verb called a Modal auxiliary is added to the verb of a sentence to indicate a particular mood of the speaker. Such a modal auxiliary is always followed by an infinitive. Sometimes a modal auxiliary is followed by a perfect infinitive to convey the speaker's attitude to a past event/situation.

Modals followed by Infinitive

2. The Modals *must* and *have* to indicate obligation /compulsion.

Examples:

(i) You must do this exercise everyday.

(ii) You have to do this exercise everyday.

Notes:

(i) The Modal *must* is never used in the past tense: instead *had to* is used.

(ii) The Modal *have* to is preferred to *must* in questions.

3. The Modal *mustn't* indicate prohibition.

Examples:

(i) You mustn't walk on the grass in the park.

(ii) He mustn't enter the campus.

Notes:

(i) The modal *mustn't/shouldn't* be mistaken for the negative of the modal *must.*

(ii) Modals in the negative are generally written with ellipsis, that is, with an apostrophe replacing the latter o in *not*, which is joined to the modal auxiliary.

4. The Modals *needn't, haven't* to, *haven't got to* and *don't have* to indicate absence of obligation and so allow a choice.

Examples:

(*i*) You needn't come with us.

(*ii*) You haven't to come with us.

(*iii*) You haven't got to come with us.

(*iv*) You don't have to come with us.

5. The Modals *can* and *could* indicate ability.

Examples:

(*i*) He can play tennis well.

(*ii*) In his younger days he could walk for hours at a stretch.

Note:

If could is used even though the context does not indicate the past, the ability indicated is rather doubtful.

Examples:

(*i*) I could perhaps help you in this task.

(*ii*) He could perhaps help us now.

6. The Modal *may* indicates permission /probability.

Examples:

(*i*) You may enter the classroom now.

(*ii*) She may buy a car next month.

7. The Modal *might* indicates probability which is somewhat uncertain.

Examples:

(*i*) I might go to Chennai to see off Radhakrishna.

8. The Modals *Should and ought* to indicate desirability /moral obligation.

Examples:

(*i*) You should respect the feelings of others.

(*ii*) You ought to obey your elders.

Modals followed by Perfect Infinitive

9. The modal *must* followed by a perfect infinitive indicate that it appears certain that something occurred.

Examples:

She is neither here nor in her brother's house; she must have gone to her sister's house in Bangalore.

10. The modal *needn't* followed by a perfect infinitive indicate that something occurred but was not necessary.

Examples:

He could have sent a telegram from Chennai; he needn't have come here.

11. The modal *could* followed by a perfect infinitive indicate that it was possible to do something which, however, was not done.

Examples:

I could have scored 100% in Mathematics if I had written the test faster.

12. The modal *may* followed by a perfect infinitive indicates that something probably happened though the speaker does not know for certain.

Examples:

Raju may have gone home upon seeing that none of us had come to the playground.

13. The modal *might* followed by a perfect infinitive indicates either (1) that something probably happened though the speaker is uncertain of it, or (2) that it was possible to do something which, however, was not done.

Examples:

(i) Ravi is neither on the playground nor in the classroom he might have gone home.

(ii) When Raja left for America he knew that I was penniless; he might have helped me.

14. The modals *should* and *ought to* followed by a perfect infinitive indicate that it was desirable/proper to do something which, however, was not done.

Examples:

(i) You should have helped that poor boy since you had a good deal of money to spare.

(ii) You ought to have attended the farewell party in Ravi since you have received a good deal of help from him.

Exercise

Fill in the blanks with suitable Modal auxiliaries.

1. You ———answer the first and the last question and any three of the other questions.

2. Policemen ———always obey their officers.
3. If you wish to smoke on the train please go to the next compartment, You ———smoke in this compartment.
4. ———I enter the classroom. sir?
5. You———visit him in the hospital very soon.
6. Your answer is full of errors. You———-be more careful.
7. I am sure you ———do much better.
8. You———not laugh at your teacher.
9. When she was barely four years old she ———recite all the multiplication tables.
10. I think we ———take an umbrella with us because it ———rain in the evening.

Scoring Key

1. You ——have to—answer the first and the last question and any three of the other questions.
2. Policemen -must———always obey their officers.
3. If you wish to smoke on the train please go to the next compartment, You —must not——smoke in this compartment.
4. May———I enter the classroom. sir?
5. You—may———visit him in the hotel.
6. Your answer is full of errors. You—should———-be more careful.
7. I am sure you —can———do much better.
8. You—can——not laugh at your teacher.
9. When she was barely four years old she -could———recite all the multiplication tables.
10. I think we -must——take an umbrella with us because it -might——— rain in the evening.

5. PASSIVE VOICE

1. In a sentence the person/thing who/which performs the action is called the Agent. The person/thing who/which suffers (that is, is the object of) the action is called this Patient.
2. If the agent who/which performs the actions is the subject of the verb, the verb is said to be in the Active voice and the sentence is called an Active sentence.

3. If the Patient who/which suffers the action is the subject of the verb, the verb is said to be in the Passive voice and the sentence is called a Passive sentence.
4. Sometimes we are more interested in an action that in who/what performed it. In such cases we use the verb in the passive voice.
5. When the agent of an action is not known the verb can be used only in the Passive voice.
6. An active sentence can be transformed into a passive sentence and vice versa.
7. The procedure for transforming an active sentence into a passive sentence is as follows.

Step (1)

Find out the verb, the subject and the object of the given active sentence.

Step (2)

Change the object of the given active sentence into its subject form and write it down.

Note:

The following table shows how to change Pronouns from the Subject form to the Object form and vice versa:

Subject	–	**Object**
I	–	me
we	–	us
you	–	you
he	–	him
she	–	her
it	–	it
they	–	them
who	–	whom
which	–	which
that	–	that

Step (3):

Add the Passive form of the verb of the given active sentence.

Notes:

(a) The Passive form of a verb is its past participle preceded by the auxiliary *be* in the appropriate tense person and number.

(b) In the Passive form of a verb the auxiliary *be* should be in the same tense as the active verb in the given active sentence.

(c) The following table gives the different tense forms of the auxiliary *be* as used in the passive form of verbs.

Simple present	–	*am/is/are*
Present progressive	–	*(am/is /are +being*
Present perfect	–	*(have/has)+ been*
Simple past	–	*was/were*
Past progressive	–	*(was/were) + being*
Past perfect	–	*had been*
Simple future	–	*(will/shall) + be*
Future perfect	–	*(will/shall)+have been*

(d) Active verb in the present perfect progressive the past perfect progressive, the future progressive and the future perfect progressive tense are not changed into the passive voice.

(e) The passive verb must always agree in person and number with the subject of the passive sentence.

Step (4)

Add the Object form of the subject of the given active sentence, preceded by the word *by.*

Examples:

1. She helps me.
   I am helped by her.
2. They help him.
   He is helped by them.
3. I help them.
   They are helped by me.
4. She is helping me.
   I am being helped by her.
5. They are helping him.
   He is being helped by them.

6. He is helping them.
   They are being helped by him.
7. She has helped me.
   I have been helped by her.
8. I have helped him.
   He has been helped by me.
9. She helped him.
   He was helped by her.
10. I helped them.
    They were helped by me.
11. She was helping him.
    He was being helped by her.
12. I was helping them.
    They were being helped by me.
13. They have helped him.
    He had been helped by them.
14. She will help us.
    We shall be helped by here.
15. I shall help her
    She will be helped by me.
16. She will have helped us.
    We shall have been helped by her.
17. I shall have helped her.
    She will have been helped by me.

Some Models

Model (1): Sentence with one Object.

Example:

They help us.

We are helped by them.

Model (2): Sentence with two Objects.

Sometimes a verb takes two objects. They are called direct object and indirect object and indirect/personal object. Either of these objects can be changed into the subject of the passive sentence. However, it is more convenient to change the indirect/personal object into the subject of the passive sentence.

Example:

Rohit gave Neela a watch.

Neela was given a watch by Rohit/A watch was given to Neela by Rohit.

Note:

Whichever of the two objects is changed into the subject of the passive sentence, the other object must be placed immediately after the passive verb in the passive sentence.

Model (3): Sentence with an Object complement.

Sometimes a sentence includes an Object complement (that is, a word/phrase that refers to the object and is necessary to complete the meaning of the sentence). When transforming such a sentence into the passive voice the object complement must be placed immediately after the passive verb of the passive sentence.

Example:

They elected him Chairman.

He was elected Chairman by them.

Model (4): Sentence with a Prepositional verb

When a sentence with a prepositional verb is transformed into the passive voice the prepositional structure of its verb should not be disturbed.

Example:

She laughed at us.

We were laughed at by her.

Model (5): Imperative Sentence:

In an imperative sentence (which expresses a command/request), the subject *you* is always implied, not expressed. When such a sentence is transformed into the passive voice, the procedure to be followed is as follows:

Step (1)

Write down the word words let/*let not* (depending upon whether the given active sentence is in the affirmative or in the negative)

Step (2)

Add the Object of the given active sentence as it is (that is without changing it into its subject form.)

Step (3)

Add the Auxiliary *be* as it is (that is, without changing into any other form).

Step (4)

Add the Past participle form of the verb of the given active sentence.

Example:

(i) Help him

Let him be helped.

(ii) Do not insult them.

Let not they are insulted.

Model (6): Interrogative Sentence:

When an Interrogative sentence (that is, a question transformed into the passive voice, the interrogative structure must be preserved.

Examples:

(i) Does he help them?

Are they helped by him?

(ii) Who helps you?

By whom are you helped?

(iii) When did they help us?

When were we helped by them?

Model (7): Tag Question.

Sometimes we wish to verify what we already know. To do this, we state what we already know and a should question called a Tag question.

Examples:

(i) He helps you, doesn't he?

(ii) She does not help them, does she?

Notes:

(i) If the statement is in the affirmative, the tag question is in the negative.

(*ii*) If the statement is in the negative, the tag question is in the affirmative.

(*iii*) In the negative tag question the word *not* is always written *n't* and joined to the auxiliary verb.

To transform a tag Question into the passive voice the following procedure is followed:

Step (1): Transform the statement into the Passive voice.

Step (2): Add a comma.

Step (3): Add the verbal 1/V, (the first auxiliary verb) of the Passive statement.

Step (4): If the passive statement is in the affirmative, add *n't* to the V

Step (5): Add the pronoun of the subject of the passive statement.

Step (6): Add the sign of interrogation (that is, the question mark).

Examples:

(*i*) He helps you, doesn't he?

You are helped by him, aren't you?

(*ii*) She does not help them, does she?

They are not helped by her, are they?

Model (8): Some Exceptional Verbs.

In the case of a few verbs the passive form of the verb is not followed by the word *by*, but by some other word, because. When used with *by*, convey special meanings.

Examples:

(*i*) I know your uncle.

Your uncle is known to me.

(*ii*) His remark surprised me.

I was surprised at his remark.

Exercise

Change the following sentences into the passive voice.

1. The dog killed the cat.
2. He does not speak the truth.
3. I do not drink coffee.
4. They never forget me.
5. I bought a hat for my brother.

6. We did not hang the picture.
7. I did not wind the clock for many days.
8. I shall choose one of these books.
9. Someone will steal your watch.
10. You should not wear this coat.

Scoring Key

1. The cat was killed by the dog.
2. Truth is never spoken by him.
3. Coffee is not drunk by me.
4. I have never been forgotten by them.
5. A hat was bought by me for my brother
6. The picture was not hung by us.
7. The clock was not wound by me for many days.
8. One of these books was chosen by me.
9. Your watch will be stolen by someone.
10. This coat should not be worn by you.

6. DEGREES OF COMPARISON

1. An Adjective is a word which describes a Noun.

Examples:

(a) She is a *good* girl.

(b) Ranjita is a *clever* girl.

2. Adjectives have three degrees of comparison. They are, Superlative, Comparative and Positive.

Examples:

(a) Ranjita is *the cleverest* girl in the class (Superlative)

(b) Ranjita is *cleverer than* any other girl in the class. (Comparative)

(c) No other girl in the class is *as clever as* Ranjita. (Positive).

3. The different degrees of comparison of every adjective should be learnt individually.
4. The superlative degree is distinguished by the combination *the* + adjective + (*st /est)* or *the* + *most* + adjective.

Examples:

(a) Ranjita is *the cleverest* girl in the class.

(b) Sobhita is *the most beautiful* girl in the class.

5. The comparative degree is distinguished by the combination adjective +(*r/er*) +*than any other* or *more* + adjective + *than any other.*

Examples:

(a) Ranjita is *cleverer than* any other girl in the class.

(b) Sobhita is *more beautiful than* any other girl in the class.

6. The positive degree is distinguished by the combination (*so /as*) + adjective + *as*.

Examples:

(a) No other girl in the class is *as clever as* Ranjita.

(b) No other girl in the class is *as beautiful as* Sobhita.

7. Sentences that compare two/more persons /things/places can be changed into the other two degrees of comparison. But sentences which compare only two persons /things /places can be changed only from comparative to positive degree and vice versa.

Some Models

Model (1):

Ritesh is the tallest boy in the class. (Superlative).

Ritesh is taller than any other boy in the class. (Comparative).

No other boy in the class is as tall as Ritesh./No other boy in the class is so tall as Ritesh. (Positive)

Model (2):

Ranjita is one of the cleverest girls in the class. (Superlative).

Ranjita is cleverer than most other girls in the class.

Ranjita is cleverer than many girls in the class. (Comparative).

Very few girls in the class are as clever as Ranjita. Very few girls in the class are so clever as Ranjita. (Positive).

Model (3):

Eritrea is not the poorest of all countries. (Superlative).

Eritrea is not poorer than some countries. (Comparative).

Some countries are at least as poor as Eritrea. (Positive).

Model (4):

Kuppam is cooler than Tirupati. (Comparative).

Tirupati is not so cool as Kuppam. /Tirupati is not as cool as Kuppam. (Positive).

Model (5):

Mumbai is not hotter than Chennai. (Comparative).

Chennai is at least as hot as Mumbai. (Positive).

Exercise

Write the other degrees of comparison for the given sentences.

1. Solomon was the wisest man of his time.
2. Helen of Troy was one of the most beautiful women.
3. Kolkotta is not the largest of all cities.
4. Ritesh is more successful than many other bowlers.
5. Kiran is not shorter than some other students.
6. America is richer than any other country.
7. Sheela is not as active as Meena.
8. Kiran is as industrious as Ramesh.
9. No other flower is as beautiful as the rose.
10. Very few buildings are as beautiful as the Taj Mahal.
11. Some boys are at least as clever as Vijay.
12. No other peak is as high as Mount Everest.
13. Very few generals were as great as Alexander.

Scoring Key

1. Solomon was the wisest man of his time.

   No other man of his time was as wise as Solomon.

   Solomon was wiser than any other man of his time.

2. Helen of Troy was one of the most beautiful women.

   No other woman of Troy was as beautiful as Helen.

   Helen was more beautiful than any other women in Troy.

3. Kolkotta is not the largest of all cities.

   No other city is as large as Kolkatta.

   Kolkatta is larger than all other cities.

4. Ritesh is more successful than many other bowlers.

   No other bowlers were as successful as Ritesh.

   Ritesh was the most successful bowler.

5. Very few generals were as great as Alexander.

   Alexander was greater than any other general.

   Alexander was the greatest among the generals.

7. REPORTED SPEECH

Direct and Reported Speech

1. Hints for changing Direct speech into Reported Speech
   1. Remove the inverted commas.
   2. Supply a suitable reporting verb and a connector
   3. Change the person of the pronouns so that the meaning of the passage remains unchanged.
   4. Change the tense of the reported verbs into corresponding past tense form.
   5. Often the simple past tense of the direct speech becomes the simple past perfect in the reported speech.
   6. A few other changes usually made are:

Now	——	then
This	——	that
These	——	those
Here	——	there
Ago	——	before
Thus	——	so
Today	——	that day
Tomorrow	——	the next day
Yesterday	——	the day before
Last night	——	the night before
Next week	——	the week after

Note:

These changes are not made if the time or the place used in the Direct Speech remains the same in the Reported Speech also.

The words of a speaker can be expressed in two ways – by quoting his active words or by reporting them indirectly. A converted sentence from Direct speech to Reported speech not only contains obvious changes in punctuation, but also in the structure of the sentence, the tense of the verb, and the forms of pronouns and adverbs used.

1. Use of noun clause beginning with that, *I* is changed to *s/he* and *tomorrow* to the *next day*. Verb changed from *present continuous* to *past continuous* tense.

   For example,

   S/he said, "I am going to Bangalore tomorrow".

   S/he said that she was going to Bangalore the next day.

2. Being a command the verb *said* is substituted by *ordered* in addition to other usual changes.

   For example,

   The Captain *said* to the soldier, "Handover your rifle to me".

   The Captain *ordered* the soldier to handover his rifle to him.

3. Being a question the verb *said* is substituted by *asked* in addition to other usual changes.

   For example,

   The teacher said to Kiran, "Have you finished your home work?"

   The teacher asked Kiran if he had finished his home work.

4. Being an exclamation the verb *said* is substituted by *exclaimed*. The words are expressed in the form of an assertion in past tense.

   For example,

   Sobhita said, "What a pretty flower this is!"

   Sobhita exclaimed that the flower was very pretty.

5. *Shall* is changed to *should, this* to *that* and *next week* to the *following week.*

   For example,

   Radhakrishna said, "I shall complete this work by next week."

   Radhakrishna said that he should complete that work by the following week.

Exercise

Change Direct speech into Reported speech.

1. Ravi said, "I have passed the Higher Secondary Course Examination"

2. Gopi said, "What are you going to do next"?
3. Ravi said, "I wanted to become an engineer once, but I am not interested in engineering any more".
4. Gopi said, "What else are you interested in"?
5. Ravi said, "I want to study English literature".
6. Gopi said, "Will you change your mind again"?
7. Ravi said, "Certainly not. Tell me what you intend to do next".
8. Gopi said, "I too am going to study English literature".
9. Gopi said, "it will be very pleasant for both of us to study the same subject".
10. Don't change your mind. I am leaving for Madras tonight and will return next week.

Scoring Key

1. Ravi told to Gopi that he had passed the Higher Secondary examination.
2. Gopi asked him what he was going to do next.
3. Ravi replied that he had wanted to become an engineer once, but was not interested in engineering any more.
4. Gopi asked him what else he was interested in.
5. Ravi answered that he wanted to study English literature.
6. Gopi asked him if he would change his mind again.
7. Ravi replied that he would certainly not and he asked Gopi to tell him what he intended to do next.
8. Gopi said that he too was going to study English literature.
9. Gopi exclaimed that it was very pleasant for both of them to study the same subject.
10. Gopi asked Ravi not to change his mind and told that he was leaving for Chennai that night and would return the week after.

8. KINDS OF SENTENCES

1. Sentences are classified into four kinds on the basis of what they do.

   The four kinds are: Assertive Sentences, Interrogative Sentences, Imperative Sentences and Exclamatory Sentences.
2. A sentence that declares/states something is called an Assertive sentence.

Examples:

(a) The moon goes round the sun as well as the earth.

(b) Ritesh has returned from Jamnagar.

Notes:

An Assertive sentence ends with a period/full-stop.

1. A sentence that asks a question is called an Interrogative sentence (question).

   Examples:

   (a) Will she come today?

   (b) Where did you go yesterday?

   (c) Who broke this plate?

Notes:

(a) The first question above can be answered with just *Yes/No.* Such interrogative sentences are called verbal questions or *Yes/No* questions.

(b) The second and the third questions above call for some information. Such interrogative sentences begin with *who, what, how, etc.* They are called pronominal questions or information questions.

(c) In interrogative sentences the word-order is important. *Yes/No* questions have the word-order V_1 +S + V_2 +...... information questions have the word-order qw (Question Word) + V_1 + S + V_2 +..... information questions beginning with *who* have the word-order *who* + V +...

(d) An interrogative Sentence ends with a question mark.

2. A sentence that expresses a request/command is called an Imperative sentence.

Examples:

(a) Help me, please.

(b) Open the door.

Notes:

(a) Imperative sentences are addressed to someone present. So in most imperative sentences the subject *you* is omitted and they begin with the verb.

(b) In imperative sentences only the infinitive is used.

(c) An imperative sentence ends with a period/full-stop.

3. A sentence that expresses some strong feeling is called an exclamatory sentence.

Examples:

(a) How beautiful the valley is!

(b) What a horrible accident!

Notes:

(a) Most Exclamatory sentences begin with *how/what* or with an exclamatory phrase consisting of either of these words followed by one/more word(s).

(b) In many exclamatory sentences the verb is omitted.

4. It is possible to change sentences from one kind to another.

Examples:

(a) She left for Bangalore yesterday. (Assertive).

When did she leave for Bangalore? (Interrogative).

(b) Open the door. (Imperative)

You are commanded to open the door. (Assertive.)

(c) What a horrible accident! (Exclamatory)

It was a very horrible accident. (Assertive).

Changing sentences from one kind to another becomes necessary when changing sentences/passages from the direct speech to the indirect or vice versa.

Exercise

Rewrite each of the following sentences as directed.

1. How cold this water is! (Into an Assertive sentence)
2. Lend me your pen, please. (Into an Assertive sentence)
3. He respects his elders (Into an Interrogative sentence beginning with *does*)
4. He will surely help us. (Into an Interrogative sentence beginning with *will*)
5. This is a very beautiful picture. (Into an Exclamatory sentence)
6. When shall we meet him? (Into an Assertive sentence, including *at 7 p.m.*)
7. Do as I tell you. (Into an Assertive sentence)
8. You are requested to keep silent. (Into an Imperative sentence)
9. We shall go to the park. (Into an Interrogative sentence beginning with *where*)

10. They returned home by bus. (Into an Interrogative sentence beginning with *how*)
11. How unlucky he is! (Into an Assertive sentence)
12. What a huge crowd! (Into an Assertive sentence)
13. This is Mary's handbag. (Into an Interrogative sentence beginning with *whose*)
14. They will return home after Diwali. (Into an Interrogative sentence beginning with *when*)
15. Do not insult the downtrodden. (Into an Assertive sentence)

Scoring Key

1. This water is very cold.
2. You are requested to give me your pen
3. Does he respect his elders?
4. Will he help us?
5. What a beautiful picture this is!
6. We shall meet him at 7 pm tomorrow.
7. You are requested to do as I tell.
8. Keep silent.
9. Where shall we go?
10. How did they return home?
11. He is very unlucky.
12. It is very huge crowd.
13. Whose hand bag is this?
14. When will they return home?
15. Let the downtrodden not be insulted.

9. SIMPLE, COMPLEX AND COMPOUND SENTENCES

1. We commonly use three different ways of constructing sentences, namely Simple, Complex and Compound. So it is common to speak of Simple sentences, Complex sentences and Compound sentences.
2. A Simple sentence is a sentence which has only one subject and one predicate.

Examples:

(a) Kiran helped Roja.

(b) Mr. Bharat is a teacher.

Notes:

(a) The Subject of a sentence is a word/phrase which refers to the person/thing/place we are speaking of in the sentence.

(b) A Predicate is a word/phrase/clause which says something (predicates) about the subject of the sentence.

3. A Complex sentence is a sentence that contains one main clause and one more subordinate clause(s).

Examples:

(a) Kiran helped Roja because he liked her.

(b) Mr. Bharat, who has moved into the house next to mine, is a teacher.

Notes:

(a) A clause is a group of words containing a subject and a predicate and forming part of a sentence.

(b) A main clause is a clause which makes complete meaning and so can, if detached from the sentence, stand by itself as a simple sentence.

Example:

Kiran helped Roja because he liked her.

(c) A subordinate clause is a clause which makes incomplete meaning and so cannot, if detached from the sentence, stand by itself.

Example:

Kiran helped Roja *because he liked her.*

4. A Compound sentence is a sentence which contains two/more main clause(s).

Examples:

(a) Kiran liked Roja and so he helped her.

(b) Ramesh studied well but he failed.

(c) Ramesh studied well and he wrote the examination well but he failed because his handwriting was so poor that the examiner was not able to read it.

5. Subordinate clause are divided into three kinds, namely Noun clauses, Adjective clauses and Adverb clauses.

6. A Noun clause is a clause that takes the place of a Noun in a sentence.

Examples:

(a) He gives us *whatever he can.*

(b) We all know *that the earth goes round the sun.*

(c) *How the thief escaped from the prison* is a mystery still.

(d) He was satisfied with *what I gave him.*

(e) Please attend to *what the teacher says.*

(f) It is certain *that he will die.*

7. An Adjective clause is a clause that takes the place of an Adjective in a sentence.

Examples:

(a) He laughs best *who laughs last.*

(b) God helps those *who help themselves.*

(c) This is the village *where he died.*

(d) This the house *that Jack built.*

(f) This is John, *whose sister we met on the train last week.*

(g) This is the messenger *whom your uncle has sent.*

(h) This is the car *which I bought yesterday.*

8. An Adverb clause is a clause that serves as an Adverb in a sentence.

9. There are nine kinds of Adverb clauses. They are Adverb clauses of

(a) Time

(b) Condition

(c) Purpose

(d) Result

(e) Concession

(f) Comparison

(g) Manner

(h) Place

(i) Reason

10. Adverb clause of Time

Examples:

(a) *When it rains heavily* we play indoor games.

(b) Look *before you* leap.

(c) *As soon as the bell rang* the students left the hall.

(d) Wait here *till he returns.*

(e) Make hay *while the sun shines.*

(f) He has not been well *since he returned from Bombay.*

11. Adverb clause of Condition.

Examples:

(a) God will forgive us *if we repent.*

(b) You will not pass *unless you study better.*

(c) *If you meet him* you will like him.

12. Adverb clause of Purpose.

Examples:

(a) We eat *that we may live.*

(b) We eat *so that we may live.*

(c) We eat *lest we should die.*

(d) We eat *in order that we mat live.*

13. Adverb clause of Result.

Examples:

(a) The news is *so* good *that it cannot be true.*

(b) This table is *so* heavy *that I cannot lift it.*

14. Adverb clause of Concession.

Examples:

(a) Though he is poor he is happy.

(b) Although she is fat she runs fast.

(c) Even though he is strong he cannot lift this table.

15. Adverb clause of Comparison.

Examples:

(a) He speaks better *than he writes.*

(b) He is as lazy *as an ass.*

16. Adverb clause of Manner.

Examples:

(a) *As you sow* so will you reap.

(b) You may do *as you please.*

(c) In Rome do *as the Romans do.*

17. Adverb clause of Place.

Examples:

(a) We go *wherever our leader takes us.*

(b) Remain *where you are.*

(c) *Where there is smoke* there is fire.

18. Adverb clause of Reason.

Examples:

(a) *Since you say so* we shall believe it.

(b) He could not come *because he was ill.*

(c) *As he was lazy* he failed.

19. A Compound sentence can be changed into a Complex sentence by converting a main clause into a subordinate clause. The process can also be reversed.
20. A Compound/Complex sentence can be changed into a Simple sentence by converting a clause in it into a word/phrase. The process can also be reversed.
21. Two/more sentences can be combined into a Simple/Complex/ Compound sentence. The process can also be reversed.
22. Two sentences can be combined into a Simple sentence by using (a) a participle (b) a preposition with a noun/gerund and (c) a nominative absolute construction.

Examples:

(a) 1. Murali was ill. He did not play.

Being ill Murali did not play. (Participle)

2. I have seen the film. I know the story.

Having seen the film I know the story. (Participle)

3. The bus overturned. It was driven by Gopal.

The bus, *driven* by Gopal, overturned. (Participle)

(b) 4. She failed many times. She continued to try.

In spite of many failures she continued to try. (Preposition with noun)

5. The sun rose. They were still sleeping.

They were sleeping *even after sunrise.* (Preposition with noun)

6. He is poor. He is contented.

   In spite of being poor he is contented. (Preposition with noun)

(c) 7. Gopal was ill. His father received us.

   Gopal being ill, his father received us. (Nominative absolute construction.)

8. The match had started. We could not enter the stadium.

   The match having started, we could not enter the stadium. (Nominative absolute construction.)

23. Two sentences can be combined into a Complex sentence by using a Noun clause/Adjective clause/Adverb clause.

Examples:

(a) Murali was ill. He did not play.

Murali, who was ill, did not play. (Adjective clause)

Since Murali was ill he did not play. (Adverb clause)

(b) He killed the merchant. He buried the body.

He buried the body of the merchant whom he had killed. (Adjective clause)

After he had killed the merchant he buried his body. (Adverb clause)

(c) I have seen the film. I know the story.

As I have seen the film I know the story. (Adjective clause)

(d) The bus overturned. It was driven by Gopal.

The bus, which was driven by Gopal, overturned. (Adjective clause)

(e) She failed many times. She continued to try.

Though she failed many times she continued to try. (Adverb clause)

(f) The sun rose. They were still sleeping.

Though the sun had risen they were sleeping. (Adverb clause)

(g) He is poor. He is contented.

Though he is poor he is contented. (Adverb clause)

(h) Gopal was ill. His father received us.

Since Gopal was ill his father received us. (Adverb clause)

(i) The match had started. We could not enter the stadium.

As the match had started we could not enter the stadium. (Adverb clause)

(j) The earth is round. We all know it.
We all know that earth is round. (Noun clause)

(k) Try again. You will succeed.
If you try again you will succeed. (Adverb clause)

(l) Children go to school. They wish to learn.
Children go to school that they may learn. (Adverb clause)

(m) The grapes were very high. The fox could not reach them.
The grapes were so high that the fox could not reach them. (Adverb clause)

(n) Iron is heavy. Lead is heavier.
Lead is heavier than Iron. (Adverb clause)

(o) You have lived so. You will die so.
You will die as you have lived. (Adverb clause)

(p) You were born in the village. Return there.
Return to the village where you were born. (Adjective clause)

24. The sets of sentences given above can be combined into Compound sentences by using conjunctions, as shown below:

(a) Murali was ill. He did not play.
Murali was ill and so he did not play.

(b) He killed the merchant. He buried the body.
He killed the merchant and he buried the body.

(c) I have seen the film. I know the story.
I have seen the film and therefore I know the story.

(d) The bus overturned. It was driven by Gopal.
The bus was driven by Gopal and it overturned.

(e) She failed many times. She continued to try.
She failed many times but she continued to try.

(f) The sun rose. They were still sleeping.
The sun had risen, yet they were still sleeping.

(g) He is poor. He is contented.
He is poor but he is contented.

(h) Gopal was ill. His father received us.
Gopal was ill and so his father received us.

(i) The match had started. We could not enter the stadium.
The match had started and so we could not enter the stadium.

(j) The earth is round. We all know it.
The earth is round and we all know it.

(k) Try again. You will succeed.
Try again and you will succeed.
Try again; otherwise, you will not succeed.

(l) Children go to school. They wish to learn.
Children wish to learn and so they go to school.

(m) The grapes were very high. The fox could not reach them.
The grapes were very high and so the fox could not reach them.

(n) Iron is heavy. Lead is heavier.
Iron is heavy but lead is heavier.

(o) You have lived so. You will die so.
You have lived so and you will die so.

(p) You were born in the village. Return there.
You were born in the village and you must return there.

25. The sets of sentences given above can also combined into Simple sentences, as shown below:

(i) Murali was ill. He did not play.
Being ill Murali did not play.
Murali did not play due to illness.
Because of illness Murali did not play.

(ii) He killed the merchant. He buried the body.
Killing the merchant, he buried the body.

(iii) I have seen the film. I know the story.
Having seen the film I know the story.

(iv) The bus overturned. It was driven by Gopal.
The bus driven by Gopal overturned.

(v) She failed many times. She continued to try.
In spite of failing many times she continued to try.

(vi) The sun rose. They were still sleeping.
They were sleeping even after sunrise.

(vii) He is poor. He is contented.

In spite of his poverty he is contented.

(viii) Gopal was ill. His father received us.

Gopal being ill his father received us.

(ix) The match had started. We could not enter the stadium.

The match having started, we could not enter the stadium.

(x) The earth is round. We all know it.

We all know the earth to be round.

(xi) Try again. You will succeed.

Trying again you will succeed.

(xii) Children go to school. They wish to learn.

Children go to school to learn.

(xiii) The grapes were very high. The fox could not reach them

The grapes were too high for the fox to reach them.

(xiv) Iron is heavy. Lead is heavier.

Between iron and lead, lead is heavier.

(xv) You have lived so. You will die so.

Your death will be like your life.

(xvi) You were born in the village. Return there.

Return to the village, the place of your birth.

Exercise

Transformation of simple sentence into a Compound sentence.

1. Ritesh should go to the railway station to receive his friends.
2. Besides getting a gold medal she also got a scholarship for her higher studies..
3. He is too weak in Maths to pass the examination.
4. Owing to financial problems he sold the house.

Transformation of a compound sentence into a simple sentence.

1. Ranjita has finished her studies and has gone abroad.
2. He has to pay the fee or he will not be allowed to write his exam.
3. You must get ready and to the bank.
4. The boat went down but the people on it were safe.

Transformation of simple sentences into complex sentences.

1. Suresh bought a red pen.
2. His success proved his efficiency.
3. Only members are allowed into the library.
5. He bought his friend's farmhouse.

Transformation of compound sentences into complex sentences:

1. He was lazy and could not be successful.
2. We must be early for the show or there will not be room for us.
3. He was denied admission and was disappointed.
4. He told the truth but nobody believed him.

Scoring Key

Transformation of simple sentence into a compound sentence.

1. Ritesh should go to the railway station and receive his friends.
2. She not only got a gold medal but also got a scholarship for her higher studies.
3. He is very weak in Maths and he cannot pass the examination.
4. He had some financial problems and therefore had to sell the house.

Transformation of a compound sentence into a simple sentence.

1. Having finished her studies, Ranjita has gone abroad.
2. He has to pay the fee to write the exam.
3. You must get ready to go to the bank.
4. In spite of the boat's going down, the people on it were safe.

Transformation of simple sentences into complex sentences.

1. Suresh bought a pen which was red.
2. His success proved that he was efficient.
3. If you are not a member, you are not allowed into the library.
4. He bought a farmhouse which belonged to his friend.

Transformation of compound sentences into complex sentences:

1. As he was lazy he could not be successful.
2. If we are not early for the show, there will not be room for us.
3. As he was denied admission, he was disappointed.
4. Although he told the truth, nobody believed him.

10. RELATIVE PRONOUNS AND CLAUSES

1. A Relative Pronoun is a word which stands for a Noun/ Pronoun already mentioned and joins different sentences/ clauses.

Examples:

Prakash is a lawyer. He is my cousin.

Prakash, who is my cousin, is a lawyer.

Notes:

(i) In the above sentence *who* is the Relative pronoun. Since it stands for *he* the pronoun *he* is called the antecedent of the Relative pronoun *Who.*

(ii) The number and the person of a Relative pronoun are always the same as those of its antecedent.

2. The most commonly used Relative pronoun are *who, whom, whose, that, which* and *what.*

Examples:

(i) Pushpa is my cousin. She is a teacher.

Pushpa, who is my cousin, is a teacher.

(ii) This letter is from Vanaja. We met her on a bus in Bangalore.

This letter is from Vanaja whom we met on a bus in Bangalore.

(iii) This cycle belongs to Ravi. His father works in a bank.

This cycle belongs to Ravi whose father works in a bank.

(iv) A boy stole your purse yesterday. This is the boy.

This is the boy that stole your purse yesterday.

(v) Radhakrishna built a house. This is the house.

This is the house that Radhakrishna built.

(vi) My watch was missing. It has been found.

My watch, which was missing, has been found

(vii) We saw a horse yesterday. I have bought it.

I have bought the horse which we saw yesterday.

(viii) You said something. I did not hear it.

I did not hear what you said.

Notes:

(i) *Who* is used in the place of subjects.

(ii) *Whom* is used in the place of objects.

(iii) *Whose* is used in the place of nouns/ pronouns in the possessive case (that is, expressing possession/ ownership?)

(iv) *That* is used in the place of subjects as well as objects

(v) *Which* is used in the place of subjects as well as objects.

(vi) *What,* when used as a Relative pronoun, means *that which.*

(vii) A Relative pronoun is generally placed as near its antecedent as possible.

Usage

3. The Relative pronoun who and whom are used only for persons.
4. The Relative pronoun whose is used for persons/animals/things.
5. The Relative pronoun which is used for animals/things.
6. The Relative pronoun that is used for persons/animals/things.
7. The Relative pronoun what is used for ideas. It is used without an expressed antecedent.
8. The Relative pronoun that is preferred.

(a) after the words all, any, only, same, much, none, nothing, few, little.

Examples:

(i) All that glitters is not gold.

(ii) Any help that is required will be given.

(iii) The only man that can help us is absent.

(iv) The same sari that we bought for Rs. 1000 in Bangalore costs Rs.1250 here.

(v) Much that was valuable was destroyed in the fire.

(vi) Nothing that you say will satisfy him.

(vii) Few that I met were ready to help me.

(viii) The little that we had was washed away in the flood.

(b) after the sequence *it is.*

Example:

It is true that we all make mistakes.

(c) after *who* and *what,* used as Interrogative pronouns.

Examples:

(i) Who that respects himself will agree to this?

(ii) What that we said displeased them?

(d) after Adjectives in the superlative degree.

Example:

This is the best that we can do.

9. When a Relative clause refers to the whole of the preceding clause and not merely to a Noun/Pronoun preceding it, only *which* is used as the Relative pronoun.

Example:

The train stopped at all stations which was very irritating.

Exercise

Join each of the following pairs of sentences by using an appropriate Relative pronoun.

1. A thief stole my purse. He has been caught.
2. He works hard. He should be encouraged.
3. I own a house. My uncle lives in it.
4. Bring me the pen. It is on the table.
5. The students have come. You wished to question them.
6. This is the knife. I carve figures with it.
7. He lent me a chair. Its legs were broken.
8. People work hard. They will surely succeed.
9. Raju is a good athlete. All his schoolmates admire him.
10. Yesterday we met Mr. Das. He is related to us.
11. Smugglers are dangerous men. The police know it.
12. You said something. Please repeat it.
13. The coach praised the captain. The captain was responsible for the victory of the team.
14. He was a brave boy. His father was proud of him.
16. Ravi is my friend. He has helped me much.

Scoring Key

1. A thief who stole my purse has been caught.
2. He, who works hard should be encouraged.

3. My uncle lives in a house which I own.
4. Bring me the pen which is on the table.
5. The students whom you wished to question have come.
6. This is the knife that I carve figures with.
7. He lent me a chair which had broken legs.
8. People who work hard will surely succeed.
9. Raju is a good athlete whose schoolmates admire him.
10. We met Mr. Das yesterday who is related to us.
11. The police know that smugglers are dangerous men.
12. Could you please repeat that you said?
13. The coach praised the captain who was responsible for the victory of the team.
14. He was a brave boy whose father was proud of him.
15. Ravi who is my friend has helped me much.

11. ARTICLES

1. Generally, every singular common noun is preceded by an Article.
2. There are three articles. They are, *a*, *an*, and *the*.
3. *A* and *an* are called Indefinite articles. They are used when we speak of any person/thing and not of a particular person/thing.

Examples:

(i) I saw a camel and an alligator in the zoo yesterday.

(ii) Early this morning I saw a beggar lying dead near an ant-hill.

4. *The* is called the definite article. It is used when we speak of a particular person/thing or of a particular group of persons/things.

Examples:

(i) Yesterday I met the Principal of your college.

(ii) He has bought the house next to mine.

(iii) The students of my class have gone on a picnic.

(iv) The houses on this street are all very small.

Usage of *a* and *an*

5. The choice between *a* and *an* is determined by the pronunciation of the word before which the article is placed.

6. *An* is used:

   1. before words beginning a vowel sound.

Examples:

(*i*) an airport

(*ii*) an entrance

(*iii*) an inch

(*iv*) an orange

(*v*) an umbrella

(*vi*) an M.L.A.

   2. before words beginning with a silent *h*.

Examples:

(*i*) an hour

(*ii*) an honour

   3. before words beginning with a *h* and not stressed on the first syllable.

Examples:

(*i*) an hotel

(*ii*) an historical figure

7. *A* is used:

   1. before words beginning with a consonant.

Examples:

(*i*) a factory

(*ii*) a locomotive

(*iii*) a machine

(*iv*) a hat

(*v*) a woman

(*vi*) a year

   2. before words beginning with a vowel which is prolonged in pronunciation, resulting in the consonant sound of *yu*.

Examples:

(*i*) a university

(*ii*) a European

3. before the words *little* and *few* when they are used to indicate a small quantity and a small number respectively.

Examples:

(*i*) A little sugar will make this dish very tasty.

(*ii*) A few boys came late to class this morning.

8. When an adjective is placed between a noun and an indefinite article, the choice between *a* and *an* is determined by the pronunciation of the adjective which is next to the article.

Examples:

(*i*) an ugly boy

(*ii*) a tasty apple

Usage of *The*

9. *The is used:*

1. When we speak of a person/thing or of a group of persons things already referred to.

Examples:

(*i*) Yesterday you introduced me to a man from Delhi. I met the man this morning in a hotel.

(*ii*) We need a particular machine for our factory. The machine is not available in India.

(*iii*) Last week we met some students from Chandigarh. The students were on a tour of South India.

(*iv*) Govind has bought ten vans. The vans have been sent to his factory in Bangalore.

2. When we speak of a particular person/thing or of a particular group of persons/things and the person we are speaking to, can clearly understand whom what we refer to.

Examples:

(*i*) I am coming from the market.

(*ii*) I have just seen off the players.

(*iii*) Let us meet the Principal.

3. before the names of things of which only one exists.

Examples:

(*i*) The sun gives us light during the day.

(*ii*) The moon gives us light during the night.

4. before the adjective *only* when it precedes a noun.

Examples:

(i) Ramesh is the only graduate in our village.

(ii) Aruna is the only lady on the Village Council.

5. before the descriptive names of countries/provinces.

Examples:

(i) the United States of America.

(ii) the United Kingdom.

(iii) the Punjab.

(iv) the Deccan.

6. before geographical terms such as the names of rivers, seas, straits, gulfs, oceans, groups of islands and mountain ranges.

Examples:

(i) the Cauvery.

(ii) the Gangas.

(iii) the Arabian Sea.

(iv) the Palk Straits.

(v) the Persian Gulf.

(vi) the Pacific Ocean.

(vii) the Andamans.

(viii) the Himalayas.

7. before adjectives in the superlative degree.

Examples:

(i) Ritesh is the best boy in the class

(ii) Sheetal is one of the cleverest girls in the class.

8. before a singular noun representing a whole class.

Examples:

(i) The dog is a faithful animal.

(ii) The donkey is a lazy animal.

Exception:

When the word *man/woman* is used to represent the whole class, *the* does not precede it.

Examples:

(i) Man is mortal.

(ii) Woman is not immortal.

9. before the names of well-known books.

Examples:

(i) the *Ramayana*.

(ii) the *Bible*.

(iii) the Qur*an*.

10. before the names of ships.

Examples:

(i) the Queen Mary

(ii) the Titanic

11. before an adjective describing a whole class.

Examples:

(i) the poor.

(ii) the wounded.

(iii) the proud.

12. When a nation (that is the people of a country) is referred to by its language.

Examples:

(i) the Japanese.

(ii) the French.

(iii) the Chinese.

Zero Articles (Omission of Article)

13. No article is used:

1. before the names of subjects of study.

Examples:

(i) We study Mathematics, Physics and Chemistry.

(ii) They study Zoology, Botany and Chemistry.

2. Before proper nouns.

Examples:

(i) I met Gopi yesterday.

(ii) We reached Mount Abu.

3. before the names of languages:

Examples:

(i) It is quite necessary to learn English.

(ii) Many Germans have mastered Sanskrit.

4. before the names of countries and towns.

Examples:

(i) Karachi is the capital of Pakistan.

(ii) Many people died in a recent storm in Indonesia.

5. before the names of days, months and seasons.

Examples:

(i) We shall return on Sunday.

(ii) It is a pleasure to visit Ooty in May.

(iii) This year summer started late.

6. before material nouns.

Examples:

(i) This ornament is made of gold.

(ii) Copper is a very useful metal.

7. before abstract nouns.

Examples:

(i) She prayed for courage.

(ii) God showed us mercy.

8. before uncountable.

Examples:

(i) She gave me advice.

(ii) She likes buttermilk.

9. before the names of places like college and market when they are visited for their primary purpose.

Examples:

(i) Ramu failed because he did not go to college regularly.

(ii) Since Sheetal goes to market everyday she knows the current price of all vegetables.

10. before the word *another.*

Examples:

(i) She wants to buy another car.

(ii) Why do you want another pen?

11. When a class of people are referred to by their religion.

Examples:

(i) Tirupati is an important place of pilgrimage for Hindus.

(ii) Vijayawada is an important place of worship for Christians.

12. before the words *little and few* when they convey a near negative meaning.

Examples:

(i) Our driver could not drive on the roads of Bangalore city because he had little experience.

(ii) The speaker ended his speech when he noticed that few members of the audience were interested in his words.

Exercise

Fill in the blanks with the appropriate Article.

1. This is ———historical event.
2. ———Cow is ———useful animal.
3. ———sun rises in ——— east and sets in ———west.
4. He is ———honourable man.
5. Raju has gone to ———market to buy fruits.
6. Many of my friends went to West Indies to find jobs only——— —few of them have found jobs there.
7. She lives in ———house next to mine.
8. In any Indian film ———hero always defeats ———Villain.
9. He looks as stupid as ———owl.
10. It was ———greatest achievement of our team.
11. ———Ganges in ———holy river.

12. Tirupati is ———important place of pilgrimage.
13. I shall return in———hour and ———half.
14. Yesterday I met ————European. He is —————only European I have ever met.
15. America is one of —————richest countries in ————world.

Scoring Key

1. This is —a————historical event.
2. The————Cow is ———a——useful animal.
3. The———sun rises in —the——— east and sets in ——the———west.
4. He is -an———honourable man.
5. Raju has gone to —the————market to buy fruits.
6. Many of my friends went to West Indies to find jobs only——a———
—few of them have found jobs there.
7. She lives in ——the——house next to mine.
8. In any Indian film —the———hero always defeats —the———Villain.
9. He looks as stupid as —an——owl.
10. It was —the————greatest achievement of our team.
11. The———Ganges is —a———holy river.
12. Tirupati is ——an——important place of pilgrimage.
13. I shall return in—an——hour and —a——half.
14. Yesterday I met —an————European. He is ——the———only European I have ever met.
15. America is one of —the————richest countries in -the————world.

12. PREPOSITIONS

A Preposition is a word which comes before a Noun or a pronoun (pre-before, position-position). It links two nouns or noun phrases.

Kinds of Prepositions

1. **Prepositions of place**

   These prepositions indicate the place of a noun, e.g. *at, in, on, inside, under, above, outside....*

2. **Prepositions of Position and Direction**

   These prepositions can either indicate positive or negative position and direction.

Positive Prepositions	Negative prepositions
In (to)	out (of)
On (to)	off
Above	below
in front of	behind
toward	away from
inside	outside

3. **Prepositions of Time**

These prepositions indicate the time of an action/event, e.g. *on, in, at, from .... to/till, during, before, after, for, since, by, until, ago...*

4. **Prepositions of Instrument/means**

These indicate the means/instrument with which an action is performed, e.g. *with* (a gun), *by* (bus),. *by means of...*

5. **Prepositions of Manner**

Manner prepositions indicate the manner in which an action was performed, e.g. *in* (a nice way), *with* (a frown).

6. **Prepositions of Agent/Doer**

They indicate the performer or doer of an action, e.g. *by* (my mother)...

7. **Prepositions of Beneficiary/Goal/Recipient**

The person who is the receiver/beneficiary is indicated by means of these prepositions, e.g. *to* (his aunt), *for* (his wife).

8. **Prepositions of Accompaniment**

They indicate the person/thing which accompanies or goes with, e.g. *with* (my mother)

9. **Prepositions of Reason/Purpose**

These indicate the reason/purpose for any action, e.g. *for* (getting first rank), *from* (fever), *because of* (his courage) ...

10. **Prepositions of Ingredient/Material**

These indicate the material with which something is made, e.g. *with* (wool), *of* (wood) ...

11. **Prepositions of Place [at, in, on]**

In general,

At refers to a position at a point /place •x

On refers to a position on a line or surface •

In refers to a position in a place that is enclosed [•]

At

(i) *At* is used to refer to a position at a point.

e.g. My institute is *at* the junction near Dravidian University.

(ii) *At* is used with the name of a place when we are interested in the activity that happens there.

e.g. There is a children's film Festival *at* Mahati Auditorium today.

(iii) *At* is used with the names of group activities.

e.g. *at* the match/*at* the function/*at* a meeting.

(iv) *At* is used with the possessive to mean "*at* somebody's place".

On

On is used to refer to a point touching a surface or close to a line.

e.g. My college is *on* the road to the University.

The boat is *on* the river.

Read the poem *on* page 34.

In

(i) *In* is used to refer to a point *in* an enclosed place.

e.g. My luggage is *in* the car.

Sobhita's clothes are *in* the wardrobe.

(ii) With larger areas (countries, states, islands) we use *in* even if they are not enclosed.

e.g. Andhra Pradesh is a State *in* India.

I have a friend *in* Andaman Islands.

(iii) We also use in to refer to pictures, sky etc.

e.g. Chiranjeevi acted *in* the film "Indian".

The plane exploded *in* the sky.

Special Uses of At. On, In

(i) Addresses

(a) With the house number: *at* is used.

e.g. I live at No. 515, Balaji Colony.

(b) With the word floor: on is used.

e.g. I live *on* the fifth floor of Balaji Towers.

(c) With the name of the street: *on/in* is used.

e.g. I live *in/on* Street No. 3, Balaji Colony.

(ii) Means of Transport

For public transport like buses and trains etc., we use *on* and *off*. for other means of transport (cars, lorries, plane) we use *in, into* and *out, out of*.

e.g. We got *off* the bus *at* Abids.

They got *into* the car and sped *off*.

We got *into* the plane just before it took *off*.

(ii) To Indicate a Target

At is used to refer to the target of some action.

e.g. smile *at* someone

laugh *at* some body

arrive *at* some place

12. Prepositions of Time

Some of the prepositions which refer to the time of an action/event are *at, in, on, from ...to, during, for, since, before, after, throughout* etc.

These prepositions can refer either to a *point of time* or a *period of time*.

At

(i) *At* is often used to refer to an exact time of an event.

e.g. The bomb exploded *at* 10 p.m. yesterday.

I get up *at* 7 a.m. daily.

(ii) *At* can also refer to part of the day/week/ year. (*at* night, *at* the weekend, *at* Christmas time).

e.g. I do my home work *at* night.

I met Aruna *at* the weekend.

It is very cold *at* Christmas time.

In

(i) *In* can refer to parts of the day.

e.g. I'll meet you *in* the evening.

I can't get up early *in* the morning.

(ii) *In* can refer to longer periods like weeks, months, years, centuries etc.

e.g. My daughter was born *in* December, *in* the year 1987.

In the nineteenth century, women hardly went out for work.

(ii) *In* can also be used to refer to the duration of an action/how soon something will happen.

e.g. The plane will arrive *in* 5 minutes.

The letter should arrive *in* 3 or 4 day's time.

On

(i) *On* is used for parts of the day (if which morning, afternoon etc. is specified).

e.g. Meet me *on* Sunday evening.

She was nervous *on* that particular night.

(ii) *On* is used to refer to particular days.

e.g. My daughter's birthday fall *on* Friday.

The Prime Minister visited Hyderabad *on* the 10th of January.

From ... To/Till/Until

To indicate when an action starts and when it finishes, we use the prepositions *from ... to/till/until*.

e.g. I request you to grant me leave *from* 15th March *to* 10th April.

The street is full of traffic *from* morning *till* night.

During

(i) *During* indicates when something happened. It stresses the period of time.

e.g. I fell sick *during* the vacation.

(ii) It can refer to an activity.

e.g. He got married *during* his training period.

Throughout

Throughout emphasizes the *entire* period of some action/event and does not refer to a particular point. It refers to long stretches of time.

e.g. I didn't study *throughout* the vacation.

(i.e. right *from* the beginning *to* the end)

Ms. Monica kept talking *throughout* the journey.

Before and After

Before and *After* refer to particular points of time.

e.g. Reach home *before* 8 o' clock.

You can leave *after* 11 o' clock.

For, Since, Ago

For is used to refer to a period of time-to say how long some action/event lasted.

Since is used to say when some action/event started. It refers to a point of time.

Ago is used to say when certain action/event in the past happened.

Since is normally used with the present perfect/past perfect tense.

For can be used with the simple present, past, present/past perfect.

Ago is used with the simple past tense.

e.g. I' ve known him *for* ten years.

My father has lived in this house *for* thirty years.

We visit Bangalore *for* a week every year.

I've known him *since* 2000.

My father bought this house 30 years *ago*.

(i) *I can concentrate and study well *in* the night.

(I can concentrate and study well *at* night.)

To refer to parts of the day, we have fixed expressions like *in* the morning, *in* the afternoon, *in* the evening but *at* night.

(ii) *The colleges are closed *in* the whole of May.

(The colleges are closed *during* the whole of May)

Though *in* and *during* refer to periods to time, there is a slight difference in meaning in certain contexts. *During* shows the duration of an event, i.e. the length of an action where as *in* says *when exactly* something happens.

So, in the above given sentence, *during* is more appropriate than *in*.

(iii) *I will be on leave *from* Monday.

(I will be on leave *from* Monday *till/to* Thursday.)

From ...... to/till forms a two – part preposition whi8ch refers to a period of time. The sentence given above is inappropriate because it does not specify the end point of the leave, in which case, the hearer would assume that the speaker has no intention of coming back to work!

(iv) *I *knew* her *since* 1999.

(I've *known* her *since* 1999.)

Since is normally used with the present/past perfect tense rather than the simple past.

(v) *I've *met* him many years *ago.*

(I *met* him many years *ago*)

Ago requires the simple past tense form of the verb. The present perfect therefore does not to with it (i.e. "ago").

(v) * He has lived in this house *since* 10 years.

(He has lived in this house *for* 10 years.)

Since refers to a specific point of time whereas *for* is used for a period of time. Since 10 years is a period, *for* is to be used instead of *since.*

(vi) *I am working here from 1997.

(I have been working here since 1997.

Since the sentence refers to an activity which began in the past and is still relevant now, the present prefect with since is to be used.

Exercise

Fill in the blanks with suitable Prepositions.

1. A bird..................hand is worth two in the bush.
2. Do not cry...................spilt milk.
3. Stella is related...................us.
4. Raju was killed......................an accident.
5. Children are fond..............sweets.
6. You ought to be ashamed...................your conduct.
7. A nurse is attending...................the patient.
8. Napoleon was defeated.................Waterloo.
9. Water consists..............hydrogen and oxygen.
10. The teacher is angry.....................him.
11. He is waiting................the results.
12. He competed..................me for the prize.
13. He has gone................. a voyage to the West Indies.
14. I am grateful..................you because you helped me.
15. I have applied.................that job.
16. You must put an end.................this bad habit.
17. Many people died.....................malaria till recently.
18. The tiger swam..................the flooded river and escaped from the hunters.

19. He has not answered..................my question.
20. I met Gopal ....my way to Madras.
21. He takes great delight.....................singing devotional songs.
22. She has done well.....................Mathematics.
23. I took pity.....................him.
24. I am not satisfied...........................your progress.
25. You should take pride.........................your achievement.
26. I have informed him......................the accident.
27. There is a great difference.....................the two models of this machine.
28. A miser will never part....................his money.
29. I paid Rs. 850................this sari.
30. Rome was not built......................a day.
31. You must get rid...................your bad friends.
32. Castor-oil is good.........................stomach ache.
33. He has applied.......................leave.
34. He is suffering........................dysentery.
35. She is studying.........................Texas.
36. The tiger pounced......................the lamb.
37. I lent him Rs.10,000 free.....................interest.'
38. Are you acquainted...........................him?
39. He is a genius, compared.......................me.
40. The hall is furnished.........................fine carpets.
41. The convict was released.........................jail.
42. He often boasts........................his wealth.
43. You must go........................a doctor immediately.
44. She reminded me...........................my promise.
45. He withdrew.............................the competition.
46. His failure was due......................his carelessness.
47. Are you for or ....this plan?
48. They congratulated us............................our victory.
49. I am obliged.........................you for your guidance.

50. We owe much.......................them.
51. Avoid the company......................bad boys.
52. Everyone in India is familiar.....................the name of Gandhi.
53. Charity begins........................home.
54. He was a great son......................India.
55. The child was delighted...........................the toy.
56. He was honored.......................his sixtieth birthday.
57. You can be proud.......................your daughter.
58. They did not agree........................me.
59. He deals.........................textiles.
60. The lorry ran ... . a child.

Scoring Key

1. A bird...in... ....hand is worth two in the bush.
2. Do not cry.........for..........spilt milk.
3. Stella is related.........to..........us.
4. Raju was killed......in................an accident.
5. Children are fond......of.........sweets.
6. You ought to be ashamed.........at...........your conduct.
7. A nurse is attending.........to..........the patient.
8. Napoleon was defeated......at...........Waterloo.
9. Water consists......of.........hydrogen and oxygen.
10. The teacher is angry......with...............him.
11. He is waiting......for..........the results.
12. He competed...with...............me for the prize.
13. He has gone.........on......... a voyage to West Indies.
14. I am grateful.........to.........you because you helped me.
15. I have applied......for...........that job.
16. You must put an end.........to.........this bad habit.
17. Many people died.........of...........malaria till recently.
18. The tiger swam...across...............the flooded river and escaped from the hunters.
19. He has not answered.........to.........my question.

20. I met Gopal ......on............my way to Bangalore.
21. He takes great delight......towards..............singing devotional songs.
22. She has done well......in..............Mathematics.
23. I took pity......on..............him.
24. I am not satisfied...........with..............your progress.
25. You should take pride.........on...............your achievement.
26. I have informed him......about...............the accident.
27. There is a great difference...between.................the two models of this machine.
28. A miser will never part......with.............his money.
29. I paid Rs.850......for..........this sari.
30. Rome was not built...........in..........a day.
31. You must get rid...........of.......your bad friends.
32. Castor-oil is good.........for...............stomach ache.
33. He has applied.........for.............leave.
34. He is suffering.........from..............dysentery.
35. She is studying...........at............Texas.
36. The tiger pounced.........upon............the lamb.
37. I lent him Rs.10,000 free...........of.........interest.
38. Are you acquainted.........with.................him?
39. He is a genius, compared.........to.............me.
40. The hall is furnished.........with................fine carpets.
41. The convict was released......from.................jail.
42. He often boasts......about.................his wealth.
43. You must go......to.................a doctor immediately.
44. She reminded me..............about............my promise.
45. He withdrew.........from....................the competition.
46. His failure was due......to...............his carelessness.
47. Are you for or ......against...................this plan?
48. They congratulated us...........at................our victory.
49. I am obliged...........to............you for your guidance.
50. We owe much......to................them.

51. Avoid the company............of..........bad boys.
52. Everyone in India is familiar.........with............the name of Gandhi.
53. Charity begins.........at..............home.
54. He was a great son......of................India.
55. The child was delighted.........at..................the toy.
56. He was absent because......of.....................illness.
57. He was honored......on................his sixtieth birthday.
58. You can be proud............of..........your daughter.
59. He deals......with...................textiles.
60. The lorry ran ... ..over.......... a child.

II. VOCABULARY

Most of the words in English are nouns, verbs, adjectives and adverbs. If one knows one form of the word one can change it into another form. For example, if one knows the word *communication* (noun) one can change it into *communicate* (verb). Similarly, if one knows the verb form of a word, one can change it into corresponding noun form.

1. Many verbs in English take -ed in the past tense and many nouns end with – tion, or-sion.

Some examples:

Verb	to	Noun
accomplish	–	accomplishment
acquaint	–	acquaintance
commit	–	commitment
conceive	–	conception
decide	–	decision
admit	–	admission
collide	–	collision
notify	–	notification
select	–	selection
apply	–	application
attest	–	attestation
register	–	registration
examine	–	examination
verify	–	verification

Noun	to	Verb
belief	–	believe
bath	–	bathe
character	–	characterize
centre	–	centralize
company	–	accompany
circle	–	encircle
colony	–	colonize
electricity	–	electrify
fool	–	befool
food	–	feed
force	–	enforce
friend	–	befriend
frost	–	freeze
furniture	–	furnish
glory	–	glorify

Exercise

Verb	Noun
to agree	agreement
to manage	---------------------
to improve	---------------------
to pay	---------------------
to amuse	---------------------
to entertain	---------------------
to perform	---------------------
to replace	---------------------
to enforce	---------------------
to imprison	---------------------
to encourage	---------------------
to employ	---------------------
to uplift	---------------------
to appoint	---------------------

to create	----------------------
to invite	----------------------
to submit	----------------------
to absorb	----------------------
to regularize	----------------------

Scoring Key

Verb	Noun
to agree	agreement
to manage	management
to improve	improvement
to pay	payment
to amuse	amusement
to entertain	entertainment
to perform	performance
to replace	replacement
to enforce	enforcement
to imprison	imprisonment
to encourage	encouragement
to employ	employment
to uplift	upliftment
to appoint	appointment
to create	creation
to invite	invitation
to submit	submission
to absorb	absorption
to regularize	regularization

Exercise

Verb	Noun
to connect	connection
to delegate	----------------------
to appreciate	----------------------
to assert	----------------------

to object	---------------------
to complete	---------------------
to destroy	---------------------
to omit	---------------------
to explain	---------------------

Scoring Key

Verb	Noun
to connect	connection
to delegate	delegation
to appreciate	appreciation
to assert	assertion
to object	objection
to complete	completion
to destroy	destruction
to omit	omission
to explain	explanation

Exercise

Noun	Verb
belief	to believe
pollution	---------------------
arrangement	---------------------
prevention	---------------------
determination	---------------------
operation	---------------------
maintenance	---------------------
constitution	---------------------
imagination	---------------------
comparison	---------------------
collaboration	---------------------
statement	---------------------
argument	---------------------
exhibition	---------------------
presentation	---------------------

Scoring Key

Noun	Verb
belief	to believe
pollution	to pollute
arrangement	to arrange
prevention	to prevent
determination	to determine
operation	to operate
maintenance	to maintain
constitution	to constitute
imagination	to imagine
comparison	to compare
collaboration	to collaborate
statement	to state
argument	to argue
exhibition	to exhibit
presentation	to present

Lexical Sets

Each topic has a set of inter-related words. Such sets are called lexical sets. Sets of words are given below and it is easy to guess the topic

(i) platform, train, compartment, coupe, berth, reservation, coolies, first class, general, A.C. sleeper, three-tier, luggage, rush, beggars, ticket collector, newspaper and magazine vendors, fruits and biscuit vendors, tea and coffee vendors, signal, announcement, arrival and departure.

(ii) hills, rivers, cattle, wells, women carrying water in mud and brass pots, crops, fields, potter, carpenter, farmer, the pipal tree, bullock carts, birds, goats, calves, kids playing, paddy, trees, plants, mud houses and roads, grocer, post-office, a hand pump.

(iii) bell, prayer, headmistress, teacher, pupil, books, time table, laboratory, library, drill, games, blackboard, classroom, test, examinations, benches, tables, duster, chalk, attendance register, uniform, literary club, reading room, maps and pictures.

Exercise

1. Give as many lexical sets of words as possible to describe a cricket match.
2. Give a lexical set of words to describe a computer.

Scoring Key

1. ball, bat, stumps, gloves, gad, captain, vice-captain, bowler, wicket, wicket keeper, runs, bowled, six, four, boundary, team-eleven members, no ball, duck out etc.
2. hard disk, monitor, screen, mouse, keyboard, mother board, server, usb cable, printer cable, printer, floppy disk, compact diskette, head phones, chipset, RAM, mega bytes, gigabytes, parallel port, scanner etc.

Antonyms and Synonyms

Each word in English has its own meaning and it can hardly be replaced by any other word. However, there are a number of words which are similar in meaning. These words are called synonyms, and learning them will help avoid repetition of the same word again and again in writing or speech. For example, complement, praise, congratulate, applaud, salute, acclaim, hail are synonymous words as they convey similar meanings.

On the other hand, antonyms are words with opposite meanings. For example, real, genuine, true and fact are antonyms of false.

Exercise

Find out the antonyms of the following words:

1. Create
2. Allow
3. Pertinent
4. Seldom
5. Praise

Scoring Key

1.	Create	x destroy
2.	Allow	x disallow
3.	Pertinent	x impertinent
4.	Seldom	x frequent
5.	Praise	x blame

Exercise

Find out the synonyms of the following words:

1. Abundant
2. Begin
3. Callous
4. Delicate
5. Effort.

Scoring Key

1. Abundant – ample, overflowing, plentiful, well-provided, well-supplied.
2. Begin- commence, start, initiate, originate, inaugurate
3. Callous – apathetic, heartless, indifferent, thick-skinned, torpid.
4. Delicate-fragile, slender, weak, frail, flimsy.
5. Effort – application, endeavour, exertion, force, power.

Collocation

Collocation refers to the occurrence of some words in the company of certain other words. For example, we say, 'commit suicide', 'commit a crime' and 'commit a blunder', but not, 'do a crime', 'do suicide' and 'do a blunder'. The combination of such words is determined by convention, and there is no rule which explains why we should not say 'do suicide'. If one wants to be a competent user of English, one must study these collocations of words carefully.

Exercise

Match the following words in accordance with appropriate collocations:

1.	cool	(a)	time	( )
2.	naked	(b)	asleep	( )
3.	fast	(c)	headed	( )
4.	tough	(d)	schedule	( )
5.	hectic	(e)	truth	( )

Scoring Key

(a) 4, (b) 3, (c) 1, (d) 5, (e) 2.

III. SPELLING

1. Words (shown in italics) which are usually misspelled.

Wrong	Right
privlege	privilege
boundry	boundary
begining	beginning
communicasion	communication
mischeivous	mischievous
recieved	received

2. Learn to spell words by syllables

A syllable is a part of a word, which such can be pronounced by itself. For example, the word later (*la□ter*) has two syllables, the word (*sacri –fice*) has three syllables, and the word *an□ti□sep□tic* has four syllables. Spellings of longer and complicated words can be learnt easily by accurately dividing the word into syllables.

Most of the words in English are disyllabic (two-syllable words) trisyllabic (three-syllable words). Words having more than three syllables may be called polysyllabic words.

For example:

Sab-bat-ic-al

Cal-cu-la-tion

Con-gra-tu-la-tions

Con-junc-ti-vi-tis

Ap-pro-xi-ma-tion

Ap-pro-pri-a-tion

Be-ne-vo-lent

Fac-sim-i-le

Im-prac-tic-able

3. Do not go by pronunciation for some spellings

We have problems with some of the peculiar sound-spelling combinations in the language.

For example

lieutenant (not leftinent)

lightning (not lightening)
perspiration (not perspirasion)
genre (not zanre)
license (not lisense)
forty (not fourty)
grammar (not grammer)
separate (not seperate)
writing (not writting)
always (not allways)

Some sounds are silent in some words. That is, the sounds are present in the spelling, but they remain silent in pronunciation.

For example: (Silent letters are in italics)

ca*l*m	si*gh*t	cou*l*d
si*g*n	cau*gh*t	solem*n*
de*b*t	shou*l*d	fi*gh*t
desi*g*n	*k*now	*k*night
*k*nit	*k*not	*k*nife
li*gh*t	*p*sychology	*p*sychiatrist

Letter 'q' is always followed by letter 'u' in any word.

For example,

quest	quantity	quit	quiet
quite	question	query	quotation
quantum	acquire	equip	equal
quiz	cheque	require	squire
square	squint	squalor	request
quarter	sequence	acquaint	equator

Spelling of the following words.

ie	**ei**
believe	freight
thief	neighbour
fierce	weight
grief	height
siege	veil
achieve	foreign

Exercise

Correct the spelling of the italicized words in the following paragraph.

Many *companys* have now *computaraised* their *acounting procejures* because computers can do the work more *quikly* and more *acuratel*y than people. The work the computer does is called data processing. The part of the computer that processes the data is called CPU (Central *Procesing* Unit). This contains the electronic *companents* called microchips.

A computer can only do what it is instructed to do. The *instrucsions* that are stored in a computer are called the computer program. The people who write these instructions are called computer *programers*.

Scoring Key

companies, computerized, accounting, procedures, quickly, accurately, processing, components, instructions, programers

IV. PUNCTUATION

1. The Commas

Some users of English have a tendency to overuse some of the marks of punctuation. For example they use the comma where it is not required. The examples given below illustrate the use of the comma:

While writing letters, the words From and To are used at the beginning to refer to the addresses of the sender and the receiver. The comma need not be placed after these two words.

*From,

From

*To,

To

In subscriptions like 'yours faithfully/sincerely/lovingly', no apostrophe (') is required after the letters 'r' in the word 'yours' as this word 'yours' is used in the way the other possessive pronouns 'theirs', 'its' and 'hers' are used with no apostrophe before –s('s).

This is yours/theirs/hers.

Yours/theirs/hers are here.

These are yours/hers/theirs.

Note that there is no indication of apostrophe before –s in all the sentences given above.

However, the comma is used after salutations (e.g. Dear Sir, Dear Bharat, etc.,) and subscriptions (e.g. your sincerely, yours lovingly, yours affectionately, etc.,)

When the word written is it's, it is abbreviated form of it is /it has.

2. Commas in Relative Clauses (Non – defining)

A clause that is marked off by commas is known as non-defining and the one that is not marked off by commas is known as the defining relative clause.

My brother who is in Delhi will come to Chennai next week (Defining Relative clause).

The sentence as it is written implies that the writer of this sentence has more than one brother. If the writer of the above sentence does not mean this, he has to change the sentence into a non-defining relative clause.

My wife, who is in Delhi, will come to Chennai next week (Non-Defining Relative clause).

3. No Commas

No commas after street numbers:

*6, Church Street *72, Gandhi Road

6 Church Street 72 Gandhi Road

Don't put a comma after the month when date and year are written.

*She was born on Sunday, July, 30 2000

She was born on Sunday, July 30 2000

4. The (full) stop (.)

Overuse of full stops:

A

Ritesh is my cousin. He is a student of class ten. He likes me. I like him. He often visits us. My father likes him. My mother likes him. We are pleased to see him.

B

Ritesh, my cousin, is a student of class ten. We like each other and my parents also like him. He often visits us and we are pleased to see him.

Passage A above consists of too many stops. Passage B that has fewer stops is a better piece of writing. Students should avoid the tendency to overuse the full stop or the period or the point.

5. No stop at the End of Addresses

There is no need to have a stop at the end of an address, whether written on the envelope or at the beginning or at the end of a personal or official letter.

*6. Marina Road, Chennai.

6 Marina Road, Chennai

No stop after common abbreviations:

*Mr. ⟶ Mr

*Mrs ⟶ Mrs

Dr. ⟶ Dr

Ms. ⟶ Ms

U.N.O ⟶ UNO

U.S.A ⟶ USA

No stops at the end of words that are abbreviated:

*exam. ⟶ Exam

*taxi. ⟶ Taxi

*maths. ⟶ Maths

*ads. ⟶ Ads

However, less common abbreviations like Ms. (for manuscript) and Ts. (for typescript) retain the stops.

6. The Colon (:)

This mark of punctuation is often used at the end of the sentence in which either the word follow or its forms 'follows'/ 'following' is used.

Examples:

The examples are as follows:

The following are the examples:

Illustrations follow:

It is also used at the end of statements like the following:

The names of the prizewinners are given below:

Colon is a mark of punctuation that balances the language units on its sides:

To err is human: to forgive divine

Sometimes what one finds before this mark of punctuation is followed by an elaboration of what has already been said.

Examples:

Optimally Useful Bilingual Dictionaries: Problems and Principles of Preparation.

India's Neighbours: Pakistan, Bangladesh, Burma, Sri Lanka, Afghanistan

Twelfth Night: Or What You Will

Note: Punctuation is a matter of practice and familiarity with the written form of English.

V. PARAGRAPH WRITING

The mastery over vocabulary and grammar should enable one to express one's thoughts accurately on any given topic. In other words, one should be able to compose different kinds of writing, like paragraphs, essays and letters on their. A good piece of writing is a combination of clear and coherent sentences presenting the topic in a logical order whether an essay or a paragraph.

Paragraph

A paragraph is a group of related sentences developed on a specific topic. It may be a part, or a division of an essay or it may be a complete unit in itself. Sometimes it is considered as a mini-essay. However, the basic difference between a paragraph and an essay is that an essay discusses many aspects of a topic, whereas a paragraph focuses on a single aspect. The paragraphs in an essay have a purpose. The beginning of a new paragraph in an essay indicates that the writer has changed the point.

A good paragraph is a combination of coherent and cohesive sentences. *Coherence* in a paragraph refers to the unity in meaning. Each sentence should be focused on the idea expressed in the paragraph. *Cohesion* refers to proper connection between one sentence and another to facilitate the reader move from one thought to another.

Features of a Paragraph

A text in which one thought or idea is developed by means of supporting details, is known as a paragraph. The supporting details can be examples, reasons, comparative statements, or other related facts. Every good paragraph has a controlling idea, to which its sentences are related.

Topic Sentence

The central idea of a paragraph can be expressed in a single sentence, which is called the topic sentence. A paragraph is built around a single idea. It is possible to make a brief statement of this idea in one sentence. This is the topic sentence or the pilot sentence. The most common pattern of the paragraph is one in which the main idea is stated first, and then explained or amplified or supported with examples or details in the sentences that follow.

There are some advantages in placing the topic sentence at the beginning of the paragraph. The writer will be able to plan the paragraph properly and prevent irrelevant material from appearing in the paragraph. The reader will know what to look for in the paragraph and will grasp the writer's point better. This arrangement, further, is a great aid to the reader who makes notes from the writing. In many paragraphs, however, one will find the topic sentence at the end.

Topic sentences are most effective, that is, they help the reader most, when they are placed at the beginning or the end of the paragraph. Sometimes, topic sentences are placed in the middle of the paragraph. They may even be implied in the paragraph: the reader will know what the central idea of the paragraph is, but will not be able to pick out any particular sentence that states the idea explicitly. With experience in writing, one will be able to introduce variety into the paragraphs by placing the topic sentence in different positions. The controlling idea of this paragraph is stated in two places. The common pattern is that the topic sentence is repeated at the end of the paragraph.

Unity

A paragraph is badly constructed if it lacks unity: that is, if it deals with more than one idea, or if it leaves the central idea half – developed. A good test of a well-written paragraph is that one can state the content of the paragraph in one sentence.

A good paragraph has unity: that is, it deals with one topic. But unity alone cannot make the paragraph effective. In a paragraph one may find that all the sentences are closely related to the central idea, but the paragraph is badly written. This happens when the sentences are not properly arranged and the reader finds it difficult to understand the inter-relation of the sentences. Then, the paragraph lacks coherence. When a paragraph is written the details should be arranged in their natural order. One sentence should lead to the next. There should be continuity and logical progression of thought.

Organization of Sentences

If a paragraph contains five facts, one can arrange them in various ways to obtain coherence. One of the simplest methods is to follow the order of time or the chronological order. The statements are placed in the order of time. This arrangement can be used in explaining process or in narrative writing.

The second possible arrangement of the sentences in a paragraph is by position or through spatial arrangement. When one follows a spatial arrangement, one can arrange material from near to far, from far to near, from outside to inside or from less prominent to more prominent.

The third method of arranging the material in a paragraph is to follow the logical order. A statement is made and then supported by means of examples; reasons are given leading to a conclusion; or a cause-and-effect relation is presented.

There are other methods of arranging the material of a paragraph: statements leading to a climax, comparison and contrast, enumeration or classification and definition. The chronological order, spatial order and logical order are the basic arrangements.

The use of Connectives

One of the means of obtaining coherence within the paragraph is to show the relation between sentences by the use of connecting words. The words used to show such relations are called connectives or transitional words. A missing connective can sometimes confuse the reader. The two sentences seem to contradict each other. But when the connective is introduced, the relation between the two sentences becomes clear. The use of connectives makes the composition clearer.

There are a few other ways of linking the sentences of a paragraph. One is the use of pronouns or other reference words. Another is the repetition of key words or sentences, sometimes slightly modified. Examples of the use of pronouns and other reference words can be easily found.

A good paragraph:

- has a central idea.
- does not contain two important ideas to confuse the reader's attention.
- is not too long.
- can also be written without a topic sentence but it is better to include one.
- has a topic sentence where it will fit logically.

Exercise

I. *The groups of sentences given below make up paragraphs. But the sentences are mixed up. Rearrange the sentences in the proper order to form good paragraphs. Sentence linking devices such as connective words or repetition of key words, which will give you a clue to the order of the sentences.*

1. (a) Vivekananda deplored such aimless assimilation of undigested knowledge.

   (b) It is something that builds character, something that brings out the divinity in man.

(c) Education today has degenerated into a purposeless accumulation of useless knowledge.

(d) Tagore too described this kind of education as "the laborious accoutrements of bookish immaturity"

(e) True education is something far different from this, something far more vital.

2. (a) Dante's vision of Beatrice is a glorification of woman.

(b) For example, Portia, in Julius Caesar, succeeds in convincing her husband, Brutus, that as his wife she has a right to know his secrets and share his anxieties.

(c) Indeed the heroines of Shakespeare's comedies are well on their way to emancipation.

(d) The Renaissance in Europe brought about a change in the concept of woman's place in society.

(e) In Shakespeare, too, there is evidence of this new attitude.

(f) This new attitude can be seen in Dante's poetry.

(g) The other Portia, the heroine of *The Merchant of Venice,* is a resourceful woman who, disguised as a lawyer, saves her lover's friend form Shylock's vengeance.

3. (a) Ordinary steel contains 0.06% to 0.12% of carbon.

(b) Stainless steel contains chromium and the steel used in making permanent magnets contains cobalt.

(c) This small quantity of carbon turns iron, which in its pure state is soft, into hard and elastic steel.

(d) Besides these common varieties of steel there are others designed by the metallurgist, which possess very special properties and answer very special needs.

(e) By the addition of elements other than carbon, we obtain steel adapted to particular uses in technology.

(f) The name steel refers to a large number of alloys of iron.

4. (a) It contains, of course, the meanings of *'difficult words'*.

(b) One of the most important reference books that you must possess is a dictionary.

(c) It also gives you the pronunciation of the words.

(d) You do possess one, perhaps, but I doubt whether you are aware of the different kinds of information it contains.

(e) Besides meaning and pronunciation, the dictionary shows you the various grammatical forms of the words.

(f) Every college dictionary should provide at least these four kinds of information about words, namely pronunciation, meaning, grammatical patterns and usage.

(g) Finally, a good dictionary contains illustrative sentences or phrases, showing how words are actually used.

5. (a) There are direct intellectual effects: the dispelling of many traditional beliefs and the adoption of others suggested by the success of the scientific method.

(b) Then, chiefly as a consequence of new techniques, there are profound changes in social organization which are bringing about corresponding political changes.

(c) The effects of science are various, of very different kinds.

(d) Then there are effects on technique in industry and war.

(e) Finally, as a result of the new control over the environment which scientific knowledge has conferred, a new philosophy is growing up, involving a changed conception of man's place in the universe.

II. *Below are some groups of sentences. In each exercise, the first sentence of a paragraph is given. That is followed by some pairs of sentences. Choose the right sentence from each pair and continue the paragraph. For example, the second sentence has to be selected from* b (i) *and* b (ii), *the third sentence from* c (i) *and* c (ii), *and so on. The first task is worked out as a model for you.*

1. (a) Humans are surrounded by a thousand enemies threatening their health, and thereby their happiness.

(b) *(i)* The World Health Organisation looks after the health of the people of the world.

(ii) Some of these enemies are so small that they cannot be seen by the unaided eye.

(c) *(i)* Nowadays there are electron microscopes which magnify objects a millionfold.

(ii) But the size of the enemy is no clue to the extent of the harm it can cause.

(d) *(i)* In fact the greatest of our enemies are the viruses and bacteria, infinitely small creatures that cause and spread some of the deadliest diseases.

(ii) A leopard, though smaller than an elephant, is a more dangerous animal.

Sentence 1 (a) shows you that the paragraph deals with health; it mentions man's enemies. Now read b (i) and b (ii). The first deals with health, and therefore has some connection with 1; the second specifically deals with man's enemies and is therefore very closely related to 1. Sentence b (ii) is to be written after 1. Suppose you wrote b (i). When you came to (c), you would find that neither c (i) nor c (ii) is related to your sentence. So you have to reject b (i). Now b (ii) says that man's enemies can be so small that they cannot be seen by the unaided eye. In (c) you have one sentence mentioning the microscope, and another continuing the idea of man's enemies. The latter seems to be a better choice, since the paragraph deals with the enemies threatening man's health. Both the sentences under (d*)* seem to continue the idea of c (ii). Which of them would you choose to preserve the unity of your paragraph? The paragraph, then, is made up of the following sentences:

Scoring Key

a, b (ii), c (ii), d (i).

Following this model, make paragraphs from the groups of sen-tences given below. The paragraph should have unity and coherence.

2. (a) People who want to climb mountains face many difficulties.

(b) *(i)* They will find it difficult to get food, since there are no hotels at such heights.

(ii) At great heights the density of the air is very low and the mountaineer will find it hard to breathe.

(c) *(i)* In modern times, therefore, mountaineers carry their own supply of oxygen in cylinders.

(ii) Not only the density of the air, but also the boiling point of water is reduced at great heights.

(d) *(i)* The cylinder adds to the weight the mountaineer has to carry, and this makes the climb arduous.

(ii) Liquid oxygen is compressed into these cylinders and then allowed to come out as a gas.

(e) *(i)* There are several other difficulties the mountaineer faces, such as unpredictable weather, treacherous sur-faces and glaciers that slide menacingly down the moun-tainside.

(ii) Therefore the mountaineer engages porters to carry some of his luggage.

(f) *(i)* Irvine and Mallory lost their lives attempting to scale Mount Everest.

(*ii*) When we remember the dangers that beset a moun-taineer, we cannot but admire the spirit that drives him to brave the unknown.

3. (a) Many people believe that it is cruel to make use of animals for laboratory studies.

(b) (*i*) The Jains, in particular, hold life to be sacred, and are therefore opposed to the use of animals in experiments.

(*ii*) These people, who have formed the Anti-Vivisection Society, have been pleading for a more humane treat-ment of animals by scientists.

(c) (*i*) They point out that animals too have nervous systems like us, and can feel pain.

(*ii*) People who supply animals to laboratories make high profits.

(d) (*i*) Monkeys, rabbits, mice and other mammals are used in large numbers by scientists, and many of them are made to suffer diseases artificially produced in them.

(*ii*) Guinea-pigs are used in laboratory experiments, and so we call a person a guinea-pig when other people use him for similar purposes.

(e) (*i*) The best solution to the problem is to stop studying animals.

(*ii*) We can avoid such cruelty to animals if we use alternative methods such as tissue culture, gas chromatography and chemical techniques.

(f) (*i*) Considerable research is being done on these techniques in different parts of the world.

(*ii*) Therefore we must become members of the Anti- Vivi--section Society.

III. *Write well□constructed paragraphs on the following topics. Use examples, arguments or explanation to amplify the statements. Discuss the topic with a partner before you start writing.*

1. The method of scoring in tennis is rather strange.
2. I have an unusual hobby. I collect bird's feathers. (You can write about any other hobby).
3. Computer games cannot provide the joy of companionship that one gets from traditional group games.
4. Television and films are responsible for the increased vio-lence in the world today.
5. One-day cricket matches are more interesting than five-day matches.

Appendix-2

Test in Writing

Marks—25

Use the words given in the brackets and frame sentences in the appropriate tense. (1m)

1. I (play) for the past four hours.
2. She (teach) since 2000.

Rewrite the following sentences using the words given in brackets. (1m)

3. No student likes to write tests. (Few)
4. They are going to Delhi. (None of)

Rewrite the sentences using the infinitives given within brackets in the appropriate tense. (1m)

5. If you start now you (reach) Bangalore by 7 p.m.
6. If they plan their trip better they (save) a good deal of money.

Fill in the blanks with suitable modals. (1m)

7. ______ I enter the classroom, Sir?
8. I am sure you ______ do much better.

Change the following sentence into active voice. (½m)

9. This coat should not be worn by you.

Change the following sentence into passive voice. (½m)

10. The dog killed the cat.

Write the other degrees of comparison for the given sentences. (2m)

11. Ranjita is the cleverest girl in the class.
12. No other girl in the class is as beautiful as Sobhita.

Change direct speech into reported speech. (½m)

13. Ranjita said, "I shall complete this work by next week".

Rewrite the following sentence into an assertive sentence. (½m)

14. How cold this water is !

Transform the following simple sentence into a complex sentence. (½m)

15. Rithesh bought a red pen.

Join the given sentences below by using an appropriate relative pronoun. (½m)

16. A thief stole my purse. He has been caught.

Fill in the blanks with the appropriate articles. (½m)

17. I saw ___ camel and ___ alligator in ___ zoo yesterday.

Fill in the blank with suitable preposition. (½m)

18. A bird _____ hand is worth two in a bush.

Give the noun form. (½m)

19. To agree

Give the verb form. (½m)

20. Belief

Fill in the blank with the adjective and identify the adverb. (½m)

21. Sobhita is a very ____________ girl.

Give the gerund form of the word in the bracket and identify the pronoun. (½m)

22. She is (play) chess.

Select the correct word out of the given choice and fill in the blank. (1m)

23. The doctor advised to ______ some rest. (have/take)

Give the corresponding antonym. (1m)

24. Construct

Give the corresponding synonym. (1m)

25. Develop

Select the correct spelling and fill in the blanks. (2m)

26. The sun _______ in the east. (raises/rises)

27. Where there is a will, _______ is a way. (there/their)

Punctuate the following sentence. (2m)

28. Sobhita said what a pretty flower this is.

Paragraph writing. (6m)

29. Write well-constructed paragraphs on "Professional Ethics for Teachers" with a Topic sentence, unity, coherence and cohesion.

Scoring Key

1. I played for the past four hours.
2. She has been teaching since 2000.
3. Few students like to write tests.
4. None of them are going to Delhi.
5. If you start now, you will reach Bangalore by 7 p.m.
6. If they plan their trip better, they would save a good deal of money.
7. _May_ I enter the classroom, Sir?
8. I am sure you _can_ do much better.
9. You should not wear this coat.
10. The cat was killed by the dog.
11. Ranjita is cleverer than any other girl in the class.
    No other girl in the class is as clever as Ranjita.
12. Sobhita is more beautiful than any other girl in the class.
    Sobhita is the most beautiful girl in the class.
13. Ranjita said that she should complete that work by the following week.
14. This water is very cold.
15. Rithesh bought a pen which was red.
16. A thief who stole my purse has been caught.
17. I saw _a_ camel and _an_ alligator in _the_ zoo yesterday.
18. A bird _in_ hand is worth two in a bush.
19. To agree - agreement
20. Belief – to believe
21. Sobhita is a very—beautiful— girl. Adverb——very.
22. She is playing chess. Pronoun——She.
23. The doctor advised to _take_ some rest.
24. Construct - destruct

25. Develop - improve
26. The sun _rises_ in the east.
27. Where there is a will, _there_ is a way.
28. Sobhita said, "what a pretty flower this is!".
29. **Professional Ethics for Teachers**

Professional ethics are the central characteristic of teaching as they are of other professions. Professional ethics cannot be imposed for by their nature they must be internalized to become part of the collective consciousness and the individual conscience. There is an unarguable case for one separate collective voice on the professional ethics of teachings and the General Teaching Council (English and Wales) is well-placed to articulate the nature of the teaching profession's collective responsibility, to initiate ongoing discussion and debate and to disseminate its findings on all aspects of professional ethics.

Sockett, (1990) said, *"Development of the model must start from start from scratch."* Comparisons with other professions do not take us very far, because the character of public interest in education differs from that for other occupations. It is to a means of achieving this shared understanding and most specifically to the arguments for the codification of professional ethics in teaching. A shared understanding and appreciation of a profession's value and ethical responsibilities are central to the profession of teaching as they are to other professions. Collective responsibility, to the client and society, based on this shared understanding is the determinant of professionalism and not autonomy.

Improvements in the morale of the teaching profession, and in the longer term improvements in motivation, expectations and standards, are dependent, in part, on an understanding and appreciation of the values and responsibilities upheld by the teaching profession, which is shared by the profession and recognized by society at large.

Reference: Meryl Thompson (1997). "Professional Ethics and the Teacher: Towards a General Teaching" England: Published by Trentham Books, Wales.

Index